**CASE STUDIES
IN CHRIST AND SALVATION**

CASE STUDIES IN CHRIST AND SALVATION

by
Jack Rogers
Ross Mackenzie
Louis Weeks

THE WESTMINSTER PRESS
Philadelphia

Book Design by Dorothy Alden Smith

Published by The Westminster Press®
Philadelphia, Pennsylvania

PRINTED IN THE UNITED STATES OF AMERICA

232.09
Rb32c
780131 4

Library of Congress Cataloging in Publication Data

Rogers, Jack Bartlett.
  Case studies in Christ and salvation.

  Includes bibliographies.
  1. Jesus Christ—History of doctrines.
2. Salvation—History of doctrines. I. Mackenzie, Ross,
1927–   joint author. II. Weeks, Louis, 1941–
joint author. III. Title.
BT198.R63   232'.09   76–53765
ISBN 0–664–24133–6

Contents

Introduction

Theology Through Cases

The chapters in this book are "case studies" written on the model developed at Harvard Business School. The authors were participants in intensive three-week training sessions at the Case Study Institute in Cambridge, Massachusetts. We are grateful to the Association of Theological Schools in the United States and Canada for its sponsorship of this Institute and to the Boston Theological Institute, the Harvard Business and Law Schools, and to our professional colleagues from theological seminaries of every denomination and geographical location for making this experience possible.

A "case," in the Harvard Business School tradition, is a write-up of an actual situation. It provides all the narrative and documentary data needed to enter vicariously into a problem. Usually the case is seen through the eyes of a person who must make an important decision. The case is left open-ended. We are not told how the issue was resolved. The reason is that the case is primarily a teaching tool. Students are asked to study the case and enter into the decision maker's experience. They are to ask themselves, What would I do?

Our task as seminary professors was to understand this method and ask ourselves how we might adapt it to our own disciplines. For some, that cross-disciplinary transfer seemed relatively simple. The decision-making context appeared to have ready application to, for example, the teaching of pastoral theology and ethics. (The first book by graduates of the Case Study Institute, *Casebook on Church and Society* (1974), contained cases that dealt with the ministry and mission of the church and with community problems.) The question remained: How useful was this decision-oriented case method in the "classical" disciplines of, for example, church history, systematic theology, and the philosophy of religion?

7

We discovered that theology is much more like business than we were willing to admit. Theological decisions are made most often in the context of practical problem-solving rather than pure theoretical speculation. Theology must "work" in the church. It must enable people to deal with their day-to-day reality. The study of church history makes this practical setting of doctrinal decisions quite clear.

On the other hand, theology has something in common with law that is largely absent from business. Business, generally, is pragmatic. The basic question is, Will it work? Law has to take another factor into account. That factor is precedent. What are the previous court decisions? Theology is like law in that respect. We too have precedents—Scripture and traditions—which must inform our decisions. A decision cannot be a "good" decision in the church unless it is both practical and placeable in the precedents on which our faith is based.

Case studies of historical situations can enable us to understand the interests and intentions of precedent makers in our traditions. Then we can lay hold of the substance of their thought and bring it to bear on new situations which they could not have foreseen. The case studies in this book are left deliberately unresolved. Often we know, or can easily discover, the outcome. Our concern is not to tell the answer, but to help the reader discover the process by which the resolution was attained. We want to understand the dynamic interaction of ancient precedents and new situations. Cases are designed to ask not just *what* happened, but *why?*

The twin themes of the book—Christ and salvation—are central to Christian experience and history. Rather than give our views, or analyze the thought of contemporary theologians, we have traced these themes through Christian history. We went to points in history where new concepts of the person of Christ or the process of salvation were conceived. We have recorded in narrative form the actual instances when these doctrines were clarified or solidified. We have also provided cases that reflect tangents proposed and rejected by the central Christian tradition.

The Divisions of This Book

Part I traces the development of the Christian church's theological understanding of the question, Who is Jesus Christ? The first four ecumenical councils of the church provide four case studies. In the fourth century, the Council of Nicaea dealt with the question of whether Jesus Christ was truly God, while the Council of Constantinople wrestled with the issue of whether Christ was truly human. In the fifth century, two further councils, Ephesus and Chalcedon, struggled to clarify the relationship of these two natures in one person. All Christian bodies affirm the essential truths of these early decisions. We have offered cases so that Christians and others can understand the intentions of the early church in the context of the philosophical, cultural, and personal milieus that gave them their form.

Part II introduces the second theme: How are we saved? Clearly the Christological element remains central. Our focus, however, is on doctrinal theories concerning the atonement. Augustine in the fifth century reflected in his teaching the earliest theories of the atonement as a ransom to Satan and a recapitulation of human life by Christ as the Second Adam. Those views continued into the Middle Ages in the person, for example, of Bernard of Clairvaux. New theories were being developed, however. Anselm enunciated the doctrine of vicarious substitution, while Abelard defended the notion of Christ's life and death as a moral influence which evoked our response. The "Abelard, Bernard, and the Council of Sens" case shows the conflict of these differing views of the atonement rooted in variant philosophies, personalities, and political circumstances.

In the period of the Protestant Reformation we have chosen particular incidents that illustrate Lutheran and Calvinist understandings of salvation over against major opponents who were proposing significantly different theories. Luther is seen in conflict with his former colleague Carlstadt, then too much aligned, Luther felt, with Anabaptist spiritualism. Calvin conflicted with Italian refugees in Geneva who anticipated the later theory of Faustus Socinus that Christ was our savior only as teacher and example. By the beginning of the seventeenth century we have three further theories of atonement. The case study of the Synod of Dort and its aftermath depicts the drama of conflict among predestinarian Calvinist, freewill Arminian, and the governmental theory of the Dutch jurist Hugo Grotius.

The case on the Shakers illustrates the introduction into America of the concept of a male/female deity and salvation through a simple and strict life under the guidance of the Spirit. Two other nineteenth-century cases highlight issues that caused significant controversies within and outside the established denominations. John McLeod Campbell was tried for heresy by the Scottish Presbyterians for affirming the universal applicability of Christ's atonement. Mary Baker Eddy's doctrines of Christian Science agitated the denominations by proclaiming a new understanding of God and a new application of salvation to physical healing.

No account of theories of the atonement would be complete without noting the twentieth-century contribution of Swedish theologian

Gustav Aulén. His "dramatic" view of the atonement depicts Christ as triumphing over sin, death, and the devil for our salvation. The case chronicles modern theological controversy occasioned by Aulén's claim that his is the "classical" view of salvation with appeals back to Luther at the Reformation and to Irenaeus in the third century.

Part III offers illustrations of contemporary contexts in which traditional views of Christ and salvation are challenged and from which perhaps new formulations will arise. The case of Kimbanguist application for membership in the World Council of Churches raises the issues of indigenization in theology and church life in the Third World. The case of Rosemary Radford Ruether records but one instance of a struggle for human liberation which is occasioning the reformulation of theological concepts of the nature of Christ and the meaning of salvation.

The last two cases depict recent international gatherings in which the meaning of Jesus Christ and the methods of salvation have been central issues. We have tried to narrate and document these events of our own recent history so that we might see them whole, but focus our attention on the twin themes of this volume. The International Congress on World Evangelization at Lausanne in 1974 and the World Council of Churches Fifth Assembly in Nairobi in 1975 raised issues and pointed directions with which we will have to deal for some time. These case studies are offered as ways by which we can enter into actual historical situations, understand their dynamics, and make our own decisions.

How a Case Is Constructed

The cases in this book are generally constructed on the model of the Harvard Business School "full text" case. With variations to suit the material, they tend to follow a four-point pattern. Part one, often a paragraph, gives the problem focus. Five items are contained in this opening section: the setting, the time, the decision maker, the specific decision to be made, and the larger issues involved. All of these are stated briefly and clearly. Thus the first few sentences should reveal what the case is about.

Part two is the exposition. It contains, usually in several paragraphs, all the facts needed as background for the case. It provides a context for the narrative to follow. It tells what people need to know in general prior to dealing with the issues.

Part three is the narrative. This is usually the longest section. It traces the development of the problem in chronological sequence.

We see the action from the perspective of one person, usually the decision maker in the case. We discover the attitudes of all who are involved as they relate to the decision maker. This narrative section culminates in a dramatic situation where the question to be decided is posed.

Part four is a brief coda or reprise. Like the problem focus at the beginning, it encapsulates the setting, time, person, and issues. It brings the case to a conclusion by pointedly posing the questions that need to be discussed in order for a decision to be made.

Sometimes case studies add a fifth section of exhibits or appendexes. We have omitted these in the interest of space, but note that documents referred to in the case usually can be acquired from standard library collections. Cross-referencing between the case and other sources will add depth to the discussion. Footnotes would disrupt the flow of involvement in the case and have been omitted in favor of a bibliography at the end of the case.

Teaching by Case Studies

These historical cases are designed primarily for classroom discussion. We hope that this book will serve as a supplementary text in seminary and college courses along with the historical or systematic treatments usually assigned. We believe that this book could also be used with profit in churches to provide material for adult courses and leadership training. The cases can be used wherever there are students seriously willing to study and discuss, and a teacher willing to prepare and enable. The following paragraphs are designed as initial guides to assist you in studying and teaching these case studies.

How the Student Should Prepare

The case method encourages cooperation rather than competition. After reading the case, students may wish to work in study groups. An hour's discussion will reveal that each person has gleaned information and formed opinions not discovered by others. In addition to discussing the case, study groups could prepare written analyses of various aspects of the case. By dividing the responsibilities, all the students in the group will be enriched by having more data or diverse points of view or collateral documents presented. It is enormously exciting when students perceive that they can learn from one another. And it is humanizing to discover that it takes the combined efforts of many to do the best job. The group interaction in class reveals that many minds working together can clarify vistas and create viable solutions that are beyond what any single individual had done.

Study groups can be helpfully employed to present the initial discussion in class. Students have developed highly creative formats for introducing a case to the whole class: panel discussions, mini-plays, TV talk-show interviews, and visuals ranging from charts, graphs, and time lines to slides and films. Study groups can become case-writing groups as well. By dividing responsibilities and sharing resources a group of five to seven students can research and write a significant case study during a quarter or a semester.

How the Case Teacher Should Prepare

The case teacher will want to prepare a "Teaching Note" prior to the class discussion. This will include several lists of data. One is an outline of the basic issues in the case. Another list is a time line, which keeps the chronology of the case clear. A cast of characters is helpful, with brief notes about each and their relationships to one another. The teacher should develop a tentative teaching plan incorporating several ideas of directions in which the case discussion could go. At times mini-lectures are effective in focusing historical material that students find "long ago and far away." Brief elucidation of particularly important or highly technical points may help to keep the discussion from becoming bogged down.

Primarily the case teacher is a discussion leader. As we prepare, we must constantly bear that in mind. Willingness and ability to be flexible and follow the class is important. The teacher is the enabler in that process. Various styles of discussion leadership will emerge, suiting the case content and the teacher's personality. Sometimes effective case leadership can appear quite authoritarian: "And what is the second meaning of salvation for Augustine?" "State precisely the four points made by the Remonstrants prior to the Synod of Dort." At other times leadership can be so democratic as to border on the anarchic: "Talk a bit among yourselves about what's going on here." "Where do we go from here?"

The central function of the teacher in any case study situation is as moderator and enabler. We ask questions. We write information on the blackboard. We make a difference depending upon what questions we ask, what responses we pick up, how we channel the conversation. We need to be sure that all relevant information is before the group. We should encourage students to interact in questioning and evaluating one another's views.

We are convinced that a wide variety of styles of case leadership will "work." The needs of the group and the authenticity of the teacher/student relationship count for more than any one way of leading the class. Some people seem more at home with patterned, forceful direction. Others function best in comparative freedom. Discerning the appropriate style, a comfortable and helpful one, is a matter for experience and sensitivity (not rules) to decide.

A General Pattern

An ideal class period would be from about ninety minutes to two hours. The first half of the period can be used to clarify the data, with the teacher asking questions and writing student responses on a chalkboard. The second half of the period can be devoted to analyzing the issues in the case and advocating and debating various points of view. That is a generally used pattern. As with any guideline, significant exceptions can be made. The "Abelard, Bernard, and the Council of Sens" case has been taught in fifty-minute adult church school class sessions spread over five Sundays. The first period was used to clarify background. Three Sundays were given to dealing with the three principal characters in turn. A final period was used to compare and contrast the positions.

Special Classroom Techniques

A wide variety of classroom techniques can be incorporated into case study sessions. The first Christological council case lends itself to role-playing. Student groups of ten and over one hundred have successfully acted out the Council of Nicaea. Subgroups can caucus to prepare the positions of Arius, Athanasius, and the middleman, Eusebius of Caesarea. The creedal formula used in Eusebius' diocese can be proposed as a motion. The case teacher can act as moderator, encouraging debate pro and con. Relevant comments often come from the larger body of bishops, ascetics, and lower clergy who make up the majority. There is always someone who can use the ego boost of being Emperor Constantine for a day and having the last word. It is astonishing how well people can imbibe the spirit of their characters and hold one another to faithfulness to the historical facts. They depart with a felt understanding of what must actually have occurred.

The Abelard case falls neatly into the use of three parallel columns for analyzing the views of the three main characters. The class can be asked for a list of questions or topics such as personality, philosophy, love life, doctrine of the atonement, lasting contribution, etc., which can be written down the left side of a chalkboard. Then each question can be posed in turn to Anselm, Abelard, and Bernard for sharp comparisons.

Cases on Luther or Calvin and their opponents encourage "embodiment." The teacher and others can come in costume as the protagonists and act out their parts fortified by historical background study to ensure authenticity.

The Shaker case was discussed after a performance by the Louisville Ballet Company at Louisville Presbyterian Seminary. That suggests the possibility of coordinating music, dance, and other art forms with the case discussion.

The Aulén case refers to numerous published articles. Students should be encouraged to read these articles and prepare analyses of them to sharpen the debate. Students could write legal briefs in defense of the position of various characters in many cases. Recently a book of cases utilizing this approach for teaching theology has been published. *Christian Theology: A Case Method Approach,* edited by Robert Evans and Thomas Parker (1976), follows the outline of the Apostles' Creed, presents brief contemporary cases, and offers several briefs in response to each case written by theologians of various persuasions.

A Third World person could be invited to class to respond to the case on Kimbanguist membership in the World Council of Churches, and to present thoughts and experience on doing indigenous theology.

Rosemary Radford Ruether could be the catalyst for opening a discussion or staging a debate on feminist theology and the role of women in the church. Probably both men and women in any class have feelings they have not voiced which might be focused through the use of this case.

The two final cases on contemporary "councils" at Lausanne and Nairobi offer an opportunity to compare modern views. Issues and emphases being advocated in the church today can be identified. Class members may be surprised to discover similarities between persons and positions they thought incompatible. At the same time, these cases might push us all to make hard choices as to where we really stand on the question of the person of Christ and the process of salvation.

All of the above are simply suggestions for the use of these cases. You will enjoy implementing your own ideas even more than following ours. Most innovative teaching techniques from programmed learning materials to simulation games can be used in combination with case studies. The heart of the matter is participation. The case is a halfway house between a totally teacher-controlled and a completely student-centered approach. The case is the common ground on which student and teacher come together and learn from each other as they make the material their own.

Appropriating History Through Cases

Our case studies are intended to be as objective as we could design them. Their open-ended style encourages the reader to resist hasty judgments. The cases in this book make no attempt to present all interpretations of events current among competent historians. We have followed prevailing schools of thought rather than introducing perspectives that are extreme. We hope the results are comparable with those found in a "textbook" representing the mainstream of current scholarship. One significant difference from most textbooks, however, is the attention to chronological sequence which the cases offer. Most historians select those events to be recorded in the light of certain interpretative interests. The case study method mandates that we be able to walk through the events with the principal decision maker. Using time sequence as the organizing principle gives the reader the opportunity to enter vicariously into the experience and do his or her own interpreting. No hypothetical situations are created. No disguises are used. The actual facts, as well as we could reconstruct them in brief compass, are presented. Normal literary license is used occasionally to create dialogue and to attribute feelings to characters. In each case we have tried to deal only with what seemed demonstrably the character's actual attitudes, even though no specific dialogue was extant.

Historical case studies can be useful to anyone who wants to deal with significant issues in their original environment. We have used the cases in this book to teach courses in philosophical theology, history of doctrine, systematic theology, and church history. They have been used with profit in doctor of ministry courses and in continuing education seminars for pastors. Lay persons taking seminary extension courses have found them an appealing alternative route to the church's history. Youth workers have discovered in them both a content and a technique which they could apply. Individuals have discovered in case studies a way to read historical theology which had the content of a textbook but the fascinating form of a detective story or a drama.

Case studies are not *the* approach to all learning. But they are a technique that has tantalizing possibilities. As these cases are used, we hope you will share the results with us. In this time of pioneering in the use of inductive teaching methods we are hoping to find further means of teaching and learning that will enrich the spiritual resources, ethical sensibilities, and sheer knowledge of us all. Too often, in education, we have given people our pre-digested results. We have thereby deprived them of the excitement of discovery which has motivated us. Our purpose in this book has been to provide facts in a form that will allow each person to make his or her own evaluation. It is because of the enjoyment, involvement, and understanding we have received in working with historical cases that we have prepared these case studies in Christ and salvation for your use.

JACK ROGERS
ROSS MACKENZIE
LOUIS WEEKS

Part I
WHO IS JESUS CHRIST?

The Christological Councils
of the Fourth and Fifth Centuries
Provide a Definition for the Church

1

The Council of Nicaea (A.D. 325) and the Question of Jesus as God

Preceded and followed by soldiers on horse or on foot, Constantine traveled the twenty miles from his imperial residence in Nicomedia to the city of Nicaea in the twentieth year of his reign. He was facing a delicate and perplexing problem—a serious division that was to involve not only the whole of the Christian church but also the very unity of his empire.

Only recently had he united the Eastern and Western regions of the empire. The eroded Rhine frontier had been restored, and the frontier garrisons rearranged and strengthened. He had put down by force his political and military foes, sending his troops into battle with the sign of his newly adopted Christian faith on their shields and banners. A political interest in the unity of his empire was dominant in his mind. But the church of his adoption had divided itself into warring factions over theological issues. At first he took the quarrel to be a mere battle of words. A unified empire demanded a unified church. But diplomatic means had failed to end the sight of Christians at verbal war with one another. So, under the guidance of what he regarded as a divine inspiration, he had summoned a universal council of the church to judge the controversy.

The city in which the bishops of the church were to meet was named, by good omen, "Victory"; and it was chosen, Constantine observed, "because of its pleasant climate." Constantine had been deeply pained: his one ecumenical empire was in jeopardy. "Disorder in the church," he said, "I consider more fearful than any other war." So, at the end of his stately procession, he entered the city of

---

This case study was prepared by Professor Ross Mackenzie of Union Theological Seminary in Virginia and Professor Jack Rogers of Fuller Theological Seminary as a basis for class discussion rather than to illustrate either effective or ineffective handling of a situation.

Nicaea on June 14, A.D. 325, to join 318 bishops of the Catholic Church to watch and to take part in the proceedings. He hoped that the decisions would resolve the theological division and bring peace to both church and empire.

Events Leading to the Council of Nicaea

As the Christian church spread and grew numerically, explaining the faith to inquirers and defending it against critics became increasingly important. Christians had not only to worship but also to think about the meaning of their faith. To bring the simple faith in God into a clear doctrinal statement was a long and hard task. The intellectual journey that was to pass through Nicaea was a search for the language by which to interpret the meaning of apostolic Christianity.

The first Christian teacher to develop a comprehensive system of thought was Origen (d. ca. 254). He interpreted the Bible on the basis of a trichotomy between the literal, moral, and spiritual meanings of the text. In his interpretation he used the concepts of Greek philosophy, especially those of Neoplatonism. So sweeping was his scope and so pioneering his effort that later students of his thought were able to develop his insights in many different directions.

One of Origen's followers was Eusebius of Caesarea (d. ca. 339). Eusebius compiled the first history of the church and became bishop of Caesarea. His history provided an apologetic for his style of leadership in the church. He pointed to two historical foci: Jesus Christ, whose deeds testified to his divinity; and Constantine, who by divine providence had opened the way for a Christian world order.

Eusebius received into his diocese a young refugee priest named Arius. Arius was a philosophical theologian who asserted that he had had to flee from Alexandria because the bishop of that place, Alexander, rejected the new scientific theology and was intolerant of differing opinions. Arius had received his theological training under Lucian of Antioch, a student of Origen. Lucian had added elements of Aristotelian rationalism to Origen's Platonic exegesis of Scripture. His strict stress on historical and grammatical method was a departure from the more allegorical exegesis of Alexandria. Like Lucian, Arius emphasized Christ's subordination to the Father. He defended monotheism as fundamental to the Christian faith, citing Deut. 6:4. A logical conclusion was that the Son was not therefore of the same nature as the Father, but was created out of nothing. Arius found Biblical support for his views in Prov. 8:22 and John 14:28.

On these grounds Arius came to oppose the bishop of his diocese, Alexander. The bishop, he argued, was advocating views akin to those of the heretic Sabellius. Sabellius had developed an aspect of Origen's thought and had spoken of God as a Monad, a single unit who reveals himself in three operations, just as the sun is itself and also radiates warmth and light. God reveals himself—the argument ran—in the Father as creator and lawgiver, and through expansion (or "dilation") expresses himself in the Son as redeemer, and in the Spirit as sanctifier. "Father," "Son," and "Spirit" are three manifestations to the world of the God who is identical in himself.

This, Arius contended, did not sufficiently differentiate between Father and Son, and sounded like the views of the heretic Paul of Samosata, who had been condemned at Antioch in A.D. 268 for teaching that Christ was "consubstantial" *(homoousios)* with the Father. Accordingly, Arius wrote to his bishop, Alexander, to explain his position. Addressing Alexander as "Blessed Pope," Arius contended that there is only one God, "unbegun and altogether sole . . . the Son being begotten apart from time . . . and was not before his generation." To the Monad he ascribed all ground of being, and therefore by definition the Logos was "of another substance" than the Father. Arius wrote in a similar vein to a friend and fellow student of Lucian, Bishop Eusebius of Nicomedia, who warmly supported him. Those who disagreed with him Arius described as heretics or "unlearned men."

Bishop Alexander of Alexandria defended his position in a letter to all the bishops of the church, criticizing Eusebius of Nicomedia and anathematizing Arius as a propounder of heresies. Alexander, as a Platonist, was particularly disturbed by the implication that the Son could change. He wrote: "How can he be mutable and susceptible of change, who says of himself, 'I and the Father are one'; and again by the Prophet, 'Behold me because I am, and have not changed'? But if anyone may also apply the expression to the Father himself, yet would it now be even more fitly said of the Word; because he was not changed by having become man, but as the Apostle says, 'Jesus Christ, the same yesterday, to-day, and forever.' " Alexander summoned a regional synod of bishops in A.D. 323, and Arius was excommunicated. Arius then traveled to Nicomedia, where he joined forces with his friend and supporter, the bishop of Nicomedia, Eusebius.

Nearly two years prior to the council, Constantine had attempted to negotiate a settlement between the major parties. He dispatched a letter to Alexandria addressed to both Bishop Alexander and Arius, expressing his impatience with what he considered a needless and senseless dispute. He offered his "imperial exhortation" to the two parties: "Indeed how few are capable either of adequately expounding, or even accurately understanding the import of matters so vast and profound! And even if anyone should be considered able to accomplish this satisfactorily, how large a portion of the people would he succeed in convincing?" Constantine urged that both parties stop the controversy, lest the people be led into "blasphemy or schism." The letter was brought to Alexandria and interpreted by Bishop Hosius of Cordova, the emperor's theological adviser. Hosius himself was steeped in the Western antiphilosophical tradition which stemmed from the Latin theologian Tertullian (ca. 160–ca. 230), whose slogan was, "What has Jerusalem to do with Athens, the Church with the Academy?" Hosius returned to Rome with a report of no progress in his discussions with Alexander and Arius. Further reports from the East told of increased strife in the church and even rioting in the streets between supporters of rival factions. Arius was reported to have a large lay following, especially among women. Popular attention had been captured for Arius' views through the use of a poem set to the tune of a bawdy song well known in the taverns:

> Arius of Alexandria, I'm the talk of all the town,
> Friend of saints, elect of heaven, filled with learning
> and renown;
> If you want the Logos doctrine, I can serve it hot and hot:
> God begat him and before he was begotten, He was not.

The Council of Nicaea

Such was the state of turbulence as the assembly met at Nicaea to debate the issues. Together with the bishops were many lower clergy, presbyters and deacons, in the church of St. Mary awaiting the arrival of the emperor. Many were scarred from the times of persecution: one with an eye put out; another tortured with a red-hot iron. There were ascetics who had spent years as hermits in forests and caves. Eusebius of Caesarea, the historian, was present. So were the principals in the conflict: Arius with his advocate, Eusebius of Nicomedia, and Alexander of Alexandria, accompanied by his theological adviser, Athanasius. Only five bishops were from the West. The aged bishop of Rome, not present, was represented by two presbyters.

The moment the approach of Constantine was announced by a given signal, all rose from their seats. "The emperor," Eusebius later wrote, "appeared like a heavenly messenger of God, covered with gold and gems, a glorious presence, very tall and slender, full of beauty, strength, and majesty." Constantine in his opening speech called on the assembly to put away all causes of strife, and prayed that the Holy Spirit might guide their counsels to a right and harmonious issue. He expressed the hope that his military victory over the tyrants might be followed by peace in the church.

It soon became plain that three main groups or parties could be discerned in the debates. The views of Arius were defended by about twenty bishops, led by Eusebius of Nicomedia. At the other extreme were the followers of Alexander, also a minority group. Their adviser was Athanasius, and they stood firm on the declaration that Jesus was of one substance with the Father. The spokesman and leader of the vast majority seemed to be Eusebius of Caesarea, who continually sought the middle ground.

Though there is no official record of the proceedings of the congress, Athanasius later clarified the stand that his side took at Nicaea. He attempted to emancipate his audience from ways of thought that conceived of God in terms of philosophy as the cause of causes, to be found by pursuing the chain of natural events. "God is not nature," he said, "nor is he the totality of its parts." God is, rather, both the source of being (Creator) and the order of the universe (Word). For Athanasius, Arianism was a form of rationalism in the guise of Christian theology. Theology, he argued, was based on the word that God addresses to mankind, and it deals in the first instance with the meaning of our salvation: "If the Son were a creature, man had remained mortal as before; for a creature had not joined creatures to God, nor would a portion of creation have been the creation's salvation, as needing salvation itself." The issue was salvation. And salvation would not have been possible had the Word been (as Arius taught) a part of creation, "for with a creature, the devil, himself a creature, would have ever continued the battle." Athanasius concluded: "For man had not been deified if joined to a creature, or unless the Son were very God."

Constantine followed the debates with intelligent interest. Proposals and counterproposals were offered to clarify the issue. Then Constantine called on Eusebius of Caesarea to propose a compromise formula. Eusebius offered a creedal statement used in his own diocese. It read:

> We believe in one God, the Father almighty, maker of all things visible and invisible.
>
> And in one Lord Jesus Christ, the Logos of God, God from God, light from light, life from life, Son only begotten, first-begotten of all creation, begotten before all ages from the Father, through Whom all things came into being, Who because of our salvation was incarnate, and dwelt among men, and suffered,

and rose again on the third day, and ascended to the Father, and will come again in glory to judge living and dead;
  We believe also in one Holy Spirit.

Constantine listened attentively as the statement was read, and approved it warmly. The bishops also responded favorably. Phrases such as "according to tradition" and "Scriptural" were heard throughout the church.

The minority party that followed Alexander proved unyielding in its opposition. The formula proposed by Eusebius of Caesarea did not deal with the problem as they saw it. Not even Arius denied that the Son was God, and the phrase "God from God" was quite acceptable to the Arians. Since, the Arians argued, all things are from God, there could be no objection to saying that the Son is from God. So the minority who supported Alexander pushed the assembly to a clearer and more precise definition.

Various amendments were proposed as the debate proceeded. One bishop suggested that the Son should be defined as "the true power and image of the Father." Others supported the phrase "in all things exactly like the Father." Winking and whispering advice to each other, the Arians accepted the amendments with no hesitation.

Only the Alexandrians were not satisfied. Constantine knew there would be no peace unless they gave their assent. Some term was needed that defined the Son and the Father as of the *same* substance. Constantine determined to propose it himself, hoping by his influence to balance the forces and arrive at a stable settlement. The relation of the Son to the Father, he said, would best be expressed by the term *homoousios* ("of the same substance").

The assembly was at once in turmoil.

2

The Council of Constantinople (A.D. 381) and the Question of Jesus as Human

After an initial flurry of excitement the bishops at Nicaea quickly acceded to the proposal of the emperor Constantine. "After our most wise and pious emperor made this philosophical statement," Eusebius recorded, "the bishops accepted the amendment." The amended creed declared that Jesus Christ, the Son of God, was "begotten not made, being of one substance *(homoousios)* with the Father." Only two bishops continued to defend Arius' position and with Arius they were excommunicated and deprived of their positions. All the others eventually subscribed the formula.

Constantine himself viewed the creed as a final and inspired statement of truth. He was confident that it would bring peace to the church and unity to the empire.

The Council of Nicaea was widely regarded as a watershed in the development of Christian teaching about Christ. It brought together many of the previous discussions about Christ's nature, some of them irreconcilable with one another. It was also likely to be, many saw, a point of reference for further developments in Christology, either in continuity with it or in opposition to it. Before long it had become a standard of what was acceptable "orthodoxy" in the greater part of the church in East and West.

Yet the Nicene victory was both superficial and incomplete. Some of the bishops had subscribed the *homoousios* formula only in deference to the emperor, or, at least, on the assumption that a broad interpretation was permissible. Others found the formula confusing. Arianism was not defeated but merely driven underground. Deep-

---

This case study was prepared by Professor Ross Mackenzie of Union Theological Seminary in Virginia and Professor Jack Rogers of Fuller Theological Seminary as a basis for class discussion rather than to illustrate either effective or ineffective handling of a situation.

seated theological divisions were sharpened by the fact that the emperor had forced the decision at the Council of Nicaea and was enforcing it in his empire. So it continued. As emperors changed their minds or were replaced by successors, new definitions of orthodoxy were enforced which often contradicted previous ones.

Events Leading to the Council of Constantinople

In the East, Arianism came to prevail. Constantine's son, Constantius, embraced the views of the excommunicated presbyter Arius with a passion. Desiring unity above all else, Constantius accepted an ambiguous confession by Arius as evidence of orthodoxy. Arius himself, therefore, was readmitted to communion two years after the Council of Nicaea. Eusebius of Nicomedia, the staunch defender of Arian views at Nicaea, was elected bishop of Constantinople. Athanasius, who succeeded Alexander as bishop of Alexandria in 328, suffered banishment for refusing to readmit Arius to the Alexandrian church. As emperors of various persuasions succeeded one another, Athanasius was forced to flee his diocese no fewer than five times.

The Western church in general was more loyal to the definition of Nicaea and regarded Athanasius as a defender of "true doctrine."

From 350 to 361 Constantius controlled the whole of the Empire and set about opposing Nicene orthodoxy with vigor. The thoroughgoing Arians surfaced and succeeded in gaining wide approval for their beliefs at a series of councils. At the Second Council of Sirmium, in 357, the Arians had the terms that were offensive to them removed:

> It is evident that there is one God, the Father Almighty, according as it is declared over the whole world; and his only-begotten Son Jesus Christ our Lord, God and Savior, begotten of him before the ages. . . . But since it troubles very many to understand about that which is termed *substantia* in Latin and *ousia* in Greek, that is to say, in order to mark the sense more accurately, the word *homoousion* (of the same substance) or *homoiousion* (of like substance), it is altogether desirable that none of these terms should be mentioned.

The rising strength of Arian extremism brought the moderate majority in the church together in order to deal with the internal dissension. At another meeting in Sirmium, called by the emperor Constantius in 358, they proposed the inclusive term *homoiousios,* saying of the Son, "God, like to the Father who begat him, according to the Scriptures." Athanasius returned from exile, and for the sake of ecumenical unity within the church, threw his support behind this position:

> Those who deny the council of Nicaea altogether are sufficiently exposed by these brief remarks; those, however, who accept everything else that was defined at Nicaea, and doubt only about the Coessential, must not be treated as enemies; nor do we attack them as Ariomaniacs, nor as opponents of the Fathers, but we discuss the matter with them as brothers with brothers, who mean what we mean, and dispute only about the word.

The Problem of Apollinarius of Laodicea

During this whole period a marked shift in the Christological controversy took place when Bishop Apollinarius of Laodicea (ca. 310–ca.390) began to apply the trinitarian results of Nicaea to Christology. The bishop was a friend and co-worker of Athanasius, and a strong supporter of the *homoousion* theology.

Theologically, Apollinarius wrestled with the question of Christ's soul (or mind) and spirit. Philosophically, he struggled with the problem of how two essences could be combined into one. His theological work produced a subtle and complex interpretation of Christ's person. As a Platonist, Apollinarius was much opposed to the Aristotelian dualism which he perceived in the Arian theology. God the Word is not one person and the man Jesus another person. He protested against those who confessed "not God incarnate, but a man conjoined with God" in a merely external union. Scripture taught that the Son of God is a unity. Anything else was philosophically inconceivable. To eliminate any dualism, Apollinarius delighted in speaking of Christ as "God incarnate," "flesh-bearing God," or "God born of a woman."

The flesh of Jesus, he contended, was joined in absolute oneness of being with the Godhead from the moment of conception. The clear assumption of his argument was that the divine Word occupied the place of normal human psychology in Christ. In the God-man, according to Apollinarius' formula, "the divine energy fulfills the role of the animating spirit and of the human mind." Unlike the Arians, Apollinarius accepted the *homoousion* formula of Nicaea. Like them, he taught that the Logos occupied the place of Christ's human spirit. But where the Arians concluded from this the changeableness of Christ, Apollinarius on the contrary concluded the unchangeableness of Christ.

The divine Word, or Logos, was the vitalizing life of the God-man, performing the functions of intellect, will, and even physical and biological energy. The advantages of this view, Apollinarius taught, were that it excluded the possibility of contradictory wills or sinful thoughts or physical passions in Christ. Christ is an organic unity. But he is such a unity because the Logos in him takes the place of the intelligent and changeable will of man. Christ is human because his body and soul are human; but he is divine because his reason is the Logos of God. Furthermore, Apollinarius shared the conviction of Athanasius that the question revolved around salvation. The divine Logos did participate in suffering, and if this had not been so, salvation would not have been possible.

> He is one nature, since he is a simple, undivided Person; for his body is not a nature by itself, nor is the divinity in virtue of the incarnation a nature by itself; but just as a man is one nature, so is Christ who has come in the likeness of men.

A group of three theologians known as the Cappadocian Fathers (Basil the Great, Gregory of Nyssa, and Gregory Nazianzen) formulated the opposition to Apollinarius. Even they proceeded with reluctance because of the brilliance of Apollinarius' arguments and the personal respect in which he was widely held.

Athanasius was also forced to join them in the fight against his old friend. He noted that in Apollinarius' teaching Christ was not a real man, but only "appeared as a man." The church, Athanasius had argued, could not accept such a docetic or apparent incarnation. Christ had a human soul and spirit. He was sad, he was in anguish, and he prayed. Gregory of Nyssa questioned the philosophical assumption that two complete entities, divinity and humanity, could not coalesce to form a real unity. Athanasius contended that rejection of a normal human psychology in Christ clashed with the Biblical picture of a Savior who developed, who was limited in knowledge, who suffered and underwent every kind of human experience. Uppermost in the concerns of Apollinarius' opponents was the advocacy of Christ as Savior. Gregory Nazianzen wrote: "If anyone has put his trust in him as a man without a human mind, he is really bereft of mind, and quite unworthy of salvation. For that which he has not assumed he has not healed; but that which is united to his Godhead is also saved."

The Council of Constantinople

In 377 and 378 the storm gathered against the opponents of Nicene orthodoxy. Apollinarianism was condemned at councils held in

Rome during the pontificate of Damasus and with the support of the powerful emperor Theodosius I. Synods in the theological centers of the East followed with condemnations at Alexandria in 378 and Antioch in 379. In 380 Theodosius issued an edict requiring his subjects to profess the "orthodox" faith of Nicaea. He raised Gregory Nazianzen to the patriarchal throne of Constantinople. Finally, he called the second ecumenical council to assemble in May, 381.

Now the weaknesses of the Nicene position were to be tested. Even Athanasius had earlier failed to say that Christ had a human soul. What needed to be said not only about Christ but also about the Holy Spirit? What was the relationship of the Spirit to the Father and to the Son? Could Christ be said to be truly human without less being said about his divinity than Nicaea had said?

The resurgent Arians, the Nicene orthodox who supported Athanasius, the moderate *homoiousians,* and the adherents of Apollinarius gathered themselves together. Like his predecessor, though with less of Constantine's diligence, the new emperor attended the sessions and showed favor to the venerable bishops. Generations later the historian Socrates Scholasticus (ca. 380–450) gave a vivid picture of the failure of the various sides to comprehend one another at the synod: "The situation was exactly like a battle at night, for both parties seemed to be in the dark about the grounds on which they were hurling abuse at each other." The Council framed no new creed or symbol, but the formula known as the Nicene Creed emerged:

We believe in one God the Father almighty, maker of heaven and earth, of all things visible and invisible;

And in one Lord Jesus Christ, the only-begotten Son of God, begotten from the Father before all ages, light from light, true God from true God, begotten not made, of one substance with the Father, through Whom all things came into existence, Who because of us men and because of our salvation came down from heaven, and was incarnate from the Holy Spirit and the Virgin Mary and became man, and was crucified for us under Pontius Pilate, and suffered and was buried, and rose again on the third day according to the Scriptures and ascended to heaven, and sits on the right hand of the Father, and will come again with glory to judge living and dead, of Whose kingdom there will be no end;

And in the Holy Spirit, the Lord and life-giver, Who proceeds from the Father, Who with the Father and the Son is together worshipped and together glorified, Who spoke through the prophets; in one holy Catholic and apostolic Church. We confess one baptism to the remission of sins; we look forward to the resurrection of the dead and the life of the world to come. Amen.

Many wondered if the new formula would be an improvement on older definitions, and if it would or could gain acceptance in the church.

3
The Council of Ephesus (A.D. 431) and the Relationship of the Two Natures in Christ

On the Day of Pentecost, A.D. 431, a third ecumenical council of the Catholic Church was convened at Ephesus. Here the pagan cult of Diana, goddess of life and light, had yielded to the Christian veneration of the Virgin Mary. The assembly, though it was to be turbulent and ridden with controversy, raised issues that were critical for the church.

Despite the earlier conflicts over differing creedal statements the vast majority of the church's teachers agreed by the end of the fourth century that Jesus Christ was both fully God and fully man. In the course of the period the two great theological traditions of the East had emerged—the schools of Alexandria and Antioch—each with a method of inquiry distinctively its own. The struggle for ecclesiastical power was complicated by the contest for supremacy between the see of Alexandria and the see of Constantinople. Two other conflicts added to the already aggravated situation. Roman emperors continued to intervene in church controversies to suit their political ends. And the pope of Rome increasingly vied with the patriarchs of the East for authority.

The theology of Apollinarius had set the stage for a conflict that was to occupy the church throughout the fifth century. The issue that had to be decided was how the divine and human natures were to be related in the one person of Christ. That issue was fought out in the struggle between two theologians of quite different temperament and outlook. Cyril, bishop of Alexandria, represented the Platonic theology of the Alexandrian school. Nestorius, bishop of Constantino-

---

This case study was prepared by Professor Ross Mackenzie of Union Theological Seminary in Virginia and Professor Jack Rogers of Fuller Theological Seminary as a basis for class discussion rather than to illustrate either effective or ineffective handling of a situation.

ple, advocated the Aristotelian theology of the Antiochene school. Was it possible for the church—many asked—to achieve clarity of meaning in defining the person of Jesus Christ and the relationship of his two natures? Or was there only one nature?

Theological Background of the Conflict

The philosophical presuppositions of the two main schools of theology became increasingly clear in the controversy over the relationship of divine and human in Christ. The Alexandrian school of thought tended to connect the human and the divine in Christ so closely that at times the human element was almost obliterated. In this school the incarnation was thought of as a mixture of human and divine.

True to the Platonic monism of the Alexandrian school Cyril sought to explain the union of the two disparate elements in Christ. His argument followed the lines of expounding two phases or stages in the existence of the Logos, the one before and the other after the incarnation. The Logos, Cyril liked to say, "remains what he was." What happened, then, at the incarnation? While continuing to exist in the form of God, the Logos added to that by taking the form of a servant. Cyril used as illustrations charcoal penetrated by fire and the union of soul and body in the human person. The clearest statement of Cyril's belief was adopted from a lately published treatise written in the name of Athanasius: "One incarnate nature of the divine Word."

The Antiochene school reflected in contrast an Aristotelian dualism. Every real entity was a combination of form and matter. There was therefore a tendency in Antiochene teachers to separate in an abstract way the two natures, divine and human, in Christ. They tended to think of the incarnation as the indwelling of the Logos in man, a moral rather than a real union between divine and human. The Antiochene theologians took as their starting point the person of Jesus, the historical figure of the Gospels, rather than the eternal Word.

The key term for them was *prosōpon*, "person," the form of the nature (or matter) of an individual being. To an Aristotelian it seemed clear that two individuals, the divine Word and the human Jesus, could come together and their two natures could appropriate a new form, or *prosōpon*, the person of Christ. This was the view of Theodore of Mopsuestia (d. 428) and his pupil, Bishop Nestorius of Constantinople (d. 451). Nestorius wrote: "We do not speak of a union of *prosōpa*, but of natures"; and again: "The two natures were united by their union in a single *prosōpon.*" According to Nestorius, "the union took place in the *prosōpon* in such wise that the one is the other and the other the one." When the Word assumed the form of a servant, the Godhead was not changed into human nature, nor was manhood deified, but these two natures were united in one personal form, Jesus Christ. It was possible, Nestorius thought, in harmony with the usage of Scripture to describe the man Jesus as God, and God the Word as man, so long as it was understood that this was a mere matter of terminology. Nestorius preferred the term "conjunction" to "union," to avoid mixing the natures. "The man" was the temple, in accordance with John 2:19, in which "the God" dwelt.

The Conflict Leading to the Council of Ephesus

On April 10, 428, Nestorius was enthroned as bishop of Constantinople. The theological difficulty for Nestorius turned upon the idea that the divine nature as such could not be born, suffer, or die. All these statements, he argued, referred not to the eternal Logos but to the man Jesus. The human nature which the Logos took in the incarnation from Mary was that of the man Jesus. So Mary was appropriately to be called Mother of Christ.

Early in his reign as patriarch, Nestorius commented on the unsuitability of a term that was coming into increasing prominence as a designation of the Virgin Mary, *theotokos* ("God-bearing," "Mother of God"). He criticized it from his pulpit as of doubtful propriety, unless *anthropotokos* ("man-bearing") was added to balance it. He much preferred the term *Christotokos* ("Christ-bearing"), because Christ was both God and man:

> No, the creature did not bear the uncreated Creator, but the man who is the instrument of the Godhead. The incarnate God did not die, but gave life to him in whom he was made flesh. This garment which he used I honor on account of the God who was covered therein and inseparable therefrom. I separate the natures but I unite the worship. He who was formed in the womb of Mary was not himself God, but God assumed him, and on account of him who assumed, he who was assumed is also called God.

Among the followers of the Alexandrian school the term *theotokos* was widely used to affirm the unity of the divinity and humanity in Jesus. Nestorius vigorously criticized its application to Mary on the grounds that it implied the Arian view that the Son was a creature, or the Apollinarian view that the manhood was incomplete. Such language, he said, could not be found in Scripture or in the confession of Nicaea. He further provoked Cyril and the Alexandrians by asserting that their phrase made Christianity appear ridiculous to nonbelievers. A woman could not carry the deity in her womb for nine months, nor could divinity suffer, die, and be buried.

As bishop of Alexandria, Cyril was jealous of the rising power of the bishopric of Constantinople. Nestorius' inflamed denial of *theotokos* to Mary gave Cyril a chance to strike. As Cyril put it, Nestorius' teaching assumed a merely moral union between the Word and an ordinary man. The incarnation thus became an illusion, an appearance, and a matter of empty words. But unless there was a real and substantial union, the redemption of mankind was nullified, since Christ's sufferings were not those of God incarnate but of a mere man. According to Cyril, the error of Nestorius could be most clearly seen when his teaching was applied to the Eucharist. If Nestorius was right, only the body of a man would lie on the altar and to eat it would be cannibalism. The flesh of Christ was not life-giving unless it was vivified by the presence of the Logos.

Cyril issued a pastoral letter at Easter, 429, devoted to refuting Nestorius' views as serious heresy. A bitter exchange of letters followed, but with no progress toward understanding. Cyril then turned to the emperor, Theodosius II (408–450), for aid against the Nestorian cause. He also made contact with Pope Celestine of Rome, sending him a dossier of selections from the sermons of Nestorius together with statements from patristic writers who contradicted Nestorius.

Celestine abruptly summoned a synod to meet at Rome in August, 430, at which the title *theotokos* was upheld and Nestorius branded as "the denier of the birth of God." On August 11 letters went out to all parties, and Nestorius was given ten days to recant or suffer excommunication. Cyril was assigned the task of carrying out the sentence.

Characteristically, Cyril went the extra mile. He held a synod of his own at Alexandria and later dispatched a lengthy letter to Nestorius with twelve articles to which Nestorius' subscription was required. The articles were deliberately provocative and set out Cyril's theology in such an extreme form that even moderate Antiochenes were shocked and alienated.

The Council of Ephesus

Nestorius appealed to the emperor for a fair hearing. On November 19, 430, Theodosius yielded and sent letters summoning a general council to meet at Ephesus on Pentecost the following year.

A group of Eastern bishops of Antiochene persuasion were delayed in arriving at the synod. Cyril with a large following of bishops convened the council under his own presidency on June 22, despite protests of the imperial commissioner. Nestorius was present at Ephesus, but refused to participate in what he considered an illegal meeting until all the bishops were present. The assembly proceeded without him to examine the disputed points and condemn and depose him in his absence. The people of Ephesus were jubilant and did great honor to Cyril.

On June 26 or the following day the Eastern bishops arrived and held a session with the approval of the imperial commissioner. They deposed Cyril and the local bishop. They also repudiated the twelve anathemas that Cyril had issued. An ugly scene of intrigue and recrimination followed.

The papal legates arrived from Rome on July 10 and reopened the whole matter on the grounds that no authoritative decision could be reached unless it was sanctioned by the bishop of Rome. This third meeting was later accepted widely as the ecumenical Council of Ephesus. The emperor at first had leaned to the side of Nestorius, but was later persuaded (by bribery, some suggested) to accept the views of the rehabilitated Cyril. Nestorius was exiled to a distant oasis, where he died in 451.

Aftermath of the Council of Ephesus

For two years following the council serious efforts were made to reconcile the divisions within the church and secure a compromise. Through the cooperation of the new pope of Rome and the emperor a formula of union proposed by John of Antioch was accepted which asserted against Cyril the duality of the two natures in Christ and against Nestorius the predicate "Mother of God." Except for the last sentence the formula was identical with a draft resolution which the Eastern bishops had approved at Ephesus in August, 431, and dispatched to the emperor Theodosius:

We confess, therefore, our Lord Jesus Christ, the only-begotten Son of God, perfect God and perfect man composed of a rational soul and a body, begotten before the ages from His Father in respect of His divinity, but likewise in these last days for us and our salvation from the Virgin Mary in respect of His manhood, consubstantial with the Father in respect of His divinity and at the same time consubstantial with us in respect of His manhood. For a union of two natures has been accomplished. Hence we confess one Christ, one Son, one Lord. In virtue of this conception of a union without confusion we confess the holy Virgin as *Theotokos* because the divine Word became flesh and was made man and from the very conception united to Himself the temple taken from her. As for the evangelical and apostolic statements about the Lord, we recognize that theologians employ some indifferently in view of the unity of person but distinguish others in view of the duality of natures, applying the God-befitting ones to Christ's divinity and the humble ones to His humanity.

Had the church found a formula of reconciliation?

4

The Council of Chalcedon (A.D. 451) and the Limits of the Doctrine of the Person of Christ

Neither the Alexandrians nor the Antiochenes were wholly satisfied with the terms of the Symbol of Union. Cyril's conservative followers were appalled by his rejection of the "one nature" *(mia physis)* and "physical union" *(henosis physike)* and his apparently willing acceptance of the doctrine of the two natures of Christ. Cyril himself was content that Nestorius had been condemned as well as the idea of a moral unity in which each nature retained its attributes. While he lived, Cyril continued to counsel moderation, and assured his followers that while the language might be objectionable, he could support the teacning.

In Constantinople the condemnation of Nestorius was widely disapproved, though the moderate Antiochenes were willing to concede Cyril's essential orthodoxy. A more extreme group persisted in asserting that it was really Cyril who was the heretic.

In A.D. 444, Cyril died and was succeeded as bishop of Alexandria by his archdeacon, Dioscorus. Dioscorus surpassed him only in ambition, aggressiveness, and ruthlessness. In intellectual ability he fell behind his predecessor. Dioscorus was determined to advance the prestige and influence of Alexandria beyond that of Constantinople. The means he chose was that of reasserting the doctrine of the one nature of Christ, which he believed Cyril had compromised in a moment of weakness.

The successor of Nestorius as bishop of Constantinople was Flavian. Flavian had espoused the strongly Eastern doctrine of the two natures. He had also a strong desire to rehabilitate the leadership

This case study was prepared by Professor Ross Mackenzie of Union Theological Seminary in Virginia and Professor Jack Rogers of Fuller Theological Seminary as a basis for class discussion rather than to illustrate either effective or ineffective handling of a situation.

of his much-criticized diocese. Many questions were in the air: What would happen to the unity of the church in the face of such division? Would the same political and theological lines simply be redrawn? Was it possible to clarify the relationship between divinity and humanity in the person of Jesus Christ?

Events Leading to the Council of Chalcedon

Tensions between the two opposing parties were brought to the surface by the case of a respected but elderly and rather confused monk named Eutyches. Like Cyril, Eutyches stressed the divine nature of Christ and denied that there were two natures after the incarnation. In Christ there was only one nature, the nature of God become man. Impersonal human nature, the argument of Eutyches ran, was assimilated by the Logos and deified in the process. But this meant that his human body could not be said to be of the same substance *(homoousios)* as that of man.

On November 8, 448, Eutyches was denounced by a local synod held at Constantinople for teaching that Christ had only one divine nature and for denying the consubstantiality of that body with those of all other human beings. Since the elderly monk enjoyed favor and influence at court, his case became a test for everyone who had some dissatisfaction with the union agreement of 433. On November 12, Flavian took the opportunity to insert into the proceedings a creedal statement in which he sought to clarify the issue: "We confess that Christ is of two natures after the incarnation, confessing one Christ, one Son, one Lord, in one *hypostasis* and in one *prosōpon.*" By identifying the terms *hypostasis* (concrete subsistence) and *prosōpon* (external aspect or form) Flavian was emphasizing his Antiochene view that personal form rather than divine or human nature was concrete individual reality.

On November 22, Eutyches appeared before the synod. He was questioned by Flavian, condemned and deposed. The heresy of Apollinarius was again invoked to identify the standpoint of Eutyches.

Eutyches thereupon wrote to Leo, bishop of Rome, appealing his case and seeking to gain support. Flavian had anticipated this strategy and had already informed Pope Leo of the condemnation. In response to the inquiries, Leo sent a theological statement to Flavian on June 13, 449. The statement came to be known as the Tome. In it Leo declared that Christ was a union of two distinct natures in one person. He inserted into the long and intricate interpretation of the discussion that was going on in the Greek church a succinct summary of Latin Christology. The key concept was that of two natures in one person. Leo wrote: "Thus the properties of each nature and substance were preserved entire, and came together to form one person." He further developed the relationship, saying: "Each nature (form, namely, of God and of servant) performs its proper functions in communion with the other; the Word performs what pertains to the Word, the flesh what pertains to the flesh. The one is resplendent with miracles, the other submits to insults."

Eutyches, on being rebuffed by Leo, turned to Dioscorus. The bishop of Alexandria in turn appealed to the emperor Theodosius II to call a general council. The council was shortly thereafter convened in Ephesus in August of 449. It was controlled by Dioscorus, and the three papal legates were prevented from reading Leo's Tome into the evidence. The phrase "after the incarnation, one nature" was declared orthodox. Eutyches, who was present and defended himself in person, was rehabilitated. The Symbol of Union of 433 was set aside as not in accordance with the doctrine of the Council of Ephesus in 431. Flavian and other exponents of the doctrine of the two natures were condemned and deposed. Flavian himself was assaulted and wounded by a band of monks. A few days later he died.

Leo branded the assembly a "Robber Synod" and appealed to Theodosius to call a new council in Italy. Since the council at Ephesus in 449 had been convened under imperial auspices, Theodosius refused to reopen the question. The impasse was broken when the emperor fell (providentially, said some) from his horse and was killed, July 28, 450.

A professional soldier, Marcian, ascended the throne and quickly solidified his position by marrying the late emperor's sister, Pulcheria. Both the new emperor and his wife sympathized with the doctrine of the two natures. It also seemed increasingly necessary to convene a new general council to settle the theological disputes and secure unity within the Empire. Leo, though he had earlier wanted to have the council convened, showed considerable reluctance to approve one now. Flavian had subscribed Leo's Tome and accepted its authority, and Leo considered the matter closed.

The Council of Chalcedon

The council was eventually convened at Chalcedon, a city opposite Constantinople. It was therefore near the capital and convenient for the emperor, his court, and the senate. The proceedings opened in the Church of St. Euphemia on a hill overlooking the Bosphorus,

October 8, 451. In number of bishops (over five hundred) who took part, it exceeded all the other ancient councils. Leo, who would have preferred to meet at Rome, was represented by a few papal legates. The imperial commissioners conducted the meetings from the front of the sanctuary screen.

From the first the business was conducted in acrimony and controversy. Fistfights were frequent. The majority of the bishops present objected to the formulation of any new creed. They simply desired to confirm the Nicene faith as the standard of orthodoxy. They affirmed the creed of the Council of Constantinople—later known as the Nicene Creed—as sufficient refutation of the heresies that arose after Nicaea. The Council next canonized with loud applause two letters of Cyril which disposed of Nestorianism. Leo's Tome was accepted as a refutation of Eutychianism with a ringing shout: "This is the faith of the fathers! This is the faith of the apostles!" The martyr Flavian was declared orthodox and Dioscorus deposed. The writings of Cyril and Leo were considered sound interpretations of the Nicene-Constantinopolitan formulation of the creed.

But even this was not sufficient for the imperial commissioners. The emperor wanted a single, enforceable definition for the whole of his empire. In response to the imperial wish the Council then produced a confession of faith:

> Following the holy fathers, we all with one accord teach men to acknowledge one and the same Son, our Lord Jesus Christ, at once complete in Godhead and complete in manhood, truly God and truly man, consisting also of a reasonable soul and body; of one substance *(homoousios)* with the Father as regards his Godhead, and at the same time of one substance with us as regards his manhood; like us in all respects, apart from sin; as regards his Godhead, begotten of the Father before the ages, but yet as regards his manhood begotten, for us men and for our salvation, of Mary the Virgin, the God-bearer *(Theotokos);* one and the same Christ, Son, Lord, Only-begotten, recognized in two natures, without confusion, without change, without division, without separation; the distinction of natures being in no way annulled by the union, but rather the characteristics of each nature being preserved and coming together to form one person *(prosōpon)* and subsistence *(hypostasis),* not as parted or separated into two persons *(prosōpa),* but one and the same Son and Only-begotten God the Word, Lord Jesus Christ; even as the prophets from earliest times spoke of him, and our Lord Jesus Christ himself taught us, and the creed of the Fathers has handed down to us.

Again the bishops exclaimed: "This is the faith of the fathers! This is the faith of the apostles!" To the creedal statement were appended condemnations of anyone who taught any different doctrine.

The final creedal statement of the Council of Chalcedon was a skillful blending of excerpts from Cyril's two letters, Leo's Tome, the Symbol of Union, and Flavian's profession of faith at the Robber Synod. But many questions remained. Could such a mélange of theologies provide a strong enough basis for the unity of the church? Had justice been done to the essential features of Alexandrian and Antiochene Christology? Had the Western or Eastern viewpoint prevailed, or had a genuine agreement been achieved? Was pope or emperor the more powerful? Above all, had the doctrine of Christ been adequately defined, with faithfulness to the Scriptural sources and reasonably to the philosophical mind?

BIBLIOGRAPHY

The following materials were used in the preparation of the Christological Councils cases and are recommended for further study.

Athanasius. *Select Works and Letters.* (Vol. IV of Select Library of Nicene and Post-Nicene Fathers, Series II.) Reprint. Wm. B. Eerdmans Publishing Company, 1971.

Bettenson, Henry, ed. *Documents of the Christian Church.* 2d ed. London: Oxford University Press, 1963.

Campenhausen, Hans von. *Fathers of the Greek Church.* Translated by Stanley Godman. Pantheon Books, 1959.

———. *The Fathers of the Latin Church.* Translated by Manfred Hoffman. Stanford University Press, 1969.

Ferm, Robert L. *Readings in the History of Christian Thought.* Holt, Rinehart & Winston, Inc., 1964.

Hardy, Edward Rochie, ed. *Christology of the Later Fathers.* (Vol. III of The Library of Christian Classics.) The Westminster Press, 1954.

Harnack, Adolf von. *History of Dogma,* Vol. IV. Translated by Neil Buchanan from the third German edition. Reprint. Dover Publications, Inc., 1961.

Kelly, J. N. D. *Early Christian Creeds.* 2d ed. London: Longmans, Green & Company, Ltd., 1960.

———. *Early Christian Doctrines.* 2d ed. Harper & Row, Publishers, Inc., 1960.

Leith, John H., ed. *Creeds of the Churches.* Rev. Ed. John Knox Press, 1973.

Lohse, Bernhard. *A Short History of Christian Doctrine.* Translated by F. Ernest Stoeffler. Fortress Press, 1966.

Pelikan, Jaroslav. *The Christian Tradition,* Vol. I. The University of Chicago Press, 1971.

Sayers, Dorothy. *The Emperor Constantine: A Chronicle.* Wm. B. Eerdmans Publishing Company, 1976.

Schaff, Philip. *The Creeds of Christendom,* Vol. I. Harper & Brothers, 1877.

Tillich, Paul. *A History of Christian Thought.* Harper & Row, Publishers, Inc., 1968.

Part II

HOW ARE WE SAVED?

*Developing Understandings in the Church
of the Meanings and Methods
of Our Salvation*

5

Augustine
and the Mercy of God (A.D. 400)

The Perplexity of Deogratias

Deogratias was perplexed. As a deacon in Carthage his task was to instruct converts and catechumens in the substance of the Christian faith. But how was he to present that truth most suitably? With what should he begin? How much should he include? With what images should he portray Christ's acts for our salvation? And should he end by pointing to practical applications, or giving a brief statement about the precepts that govern the Christian way of life?

In a letter Deogratias laid his difficulties before Augustine, the bishop of Hippo. With the generosity typical of his nature Augustine responded to the deacon by composing a book, *Instruction for Beginners.* The advice in the *Instruction* was clear: Tell your hearers a little at a time, but tell it well; tell it as a story, the account of how God has dealt with us from the beginning until now; and tell it so that those who hear may learn that they are loved by God.

The writer of the advice had had much experience in instructing converts and teaching the Christian faith to the congregations that thronged the Great Church in Hippo.

Around the year A.D. 400 the coastal strip of Africa was a wealthy and heavily populated region. The harbor town of Hippo, enfolded by a curve in the coastline, was indistinguishable from many other Mediterranean towns and ports. Dirty white houses rose steeply from the sea. On one side the forum was overshadowed by cult temples; on the other it opened out to the noisy porticoed bazaars.

This case study was prepared by Professor Ross Mackenzie of Union Theological Seminary in Virginia as a basis for class discussion rather than to illustrate either effective or ineffective handling of a situation.

A well-adorned theater was close by, and a stadium in which musicians, pantomimists, artists, and charioteers provided entertainment.

Hippo also contained the Great Church, the *basilica major*, with its baptistery and adjoining devotional chapel for the relics of St. Stephen. Among the buildings were the bishop's palace and a little monastery which housed a community of monks under the leadership of their bishop.

Some Strange Ideas of the Inhabitants of Hippo

In the basilica Augustine preached to his monks and people. He was seated on a marble chair on the dais of the apse, or, when the church was thronged, he stood upright on the top step of the apse. The people followed his words and arguments with lively interest, laughter, applause, and even at times conversation with him. Augustine knew his people well and they knew his favorite texts by heart, and what were his favorite chapters in the Bible.

In the reception room he met with those who were preparing in a more intimate atmosphere for reception into the Catholic Church. He always asked why they were seeking instruction. It was a delicate moment, for he knew that their motives were mixed and their minds confused by strange ideas. Many told him how they used astrology to forecast the outcome of their acts. He gently rebuked them; but he was well aware that some of them were saying: "I will not start on my journey, because it is an unlucky day" or "because the moon is in such a quarter," or "I will start, because the position of the stars guarantees luck." "I will not carry on business this month, because that star works against me," or "I will carry on, because it favors the month," or "I will not plant a vineyard this year because it is leap year."

The desire to foretell the future, Augustine explained to his people, is a grave error, a deceitful folly: "A Christian must completely reject and shun all the arts of a superstition like this." Astrology was part of the legacy of paganism, an apparatus used by the demons to deceive the simple and credulous, an instrument of seduction: "In all these sciences, therefore, we must dread and avoid association with demons, who strive, along with the Devil their leader, solely to block and cut off our way back home."

The Death That Overcame the Devil

In one of his Ascension sermons Augustine spoke to his people about the meaning of salvation as Christ's defeat of the devil:

We have our Lord and Savior Jesus Christ hanging on a cross, now enthroned in heaven. He paid our price when he hung upon the cross; he gathers what he purchased when he sits enthroned in heaven.

If he had not been put to death, death would not have died. The Devil was overcome by his own trophy, for the Devil rejoiced when, by seducing the first man, he cast him into death. By seducing the first man, he killed him; by killing the last Man, he lost the first from his snare.

The Apostle Peter says, "It is necessary for you to be on your guard against temptations, for your adversary the devil goes about seeking someone to devour." Who would be safe from the teeth of this lion if the Lion of the tribe of Juda had not prevailed? The Lion stood against the lion; the Lamb against the wolf. The Devil exulted when Christ died, and by that very death of Christ the Devil was overcome: he took food, as it were, from a trap. He gloated over the death as if he were appointed a deputy of death; that in which he rejoiced became a prison for him. The cross of the Lord became a trap for the Devil; the death of the Lord was the food by which he was ensnared. And behold, our Lord Jesus Christ rose again. Where is the death which hung upon the cross?

On this day, as you have heard, our Lord Jesus Christ ascended into heaven; may our hearts, too, ascend with him. Let us hearken to the Apostle when he says: "If you have risen with Christ, seek the things that are above, where Christ is seated at the right hand of God. Mind the things that are above, not the things that are on the earth." For, just as he ascended into heaven without departing from us, so we, too, are already there with him although that which he promised us has not yet been accomplished in our body. He has already been exalted above the heavens.

On earth let us meditate on that which we look forward to in heaven. Then we shall put off the flesh of mortality; now let us put aside the sluggishness of our mind. The body will easily be lifted to the heights of heaven if the weight of our sins does not press down upon our spirit.

In another of his sermons the bishop of Hippo explained the role of Christ's humanity in his work of salvation:

From what he has of himself he is the Son of God; from what he has of us he is the Son of man. He has received the lesser part from us; he has given us the greater part. For he also died because he is the Son of man, not because he is the Son of God. Nevertheless the Son of God died, although he died according to the flesh and not according to the Word. . . . Therefore because he died, he died of what he had of us; because we live, we live from what we have of him.

And for us, what does it mean that Jesus Christ has died? In one of his Lenten sermons Augustine interpreted his understanding of a Pauline text:

> "And they who belong to Christ have crucified their flesh with its passions and desires" (Gal. 5:24). In fact, the Christian ought to be suspended constantly on this cross through his entire life, passed as it is in the midst of temptation. For there is no time in this life when we can tear out the nails of which the Psalmist speaks in the words: "Pierce thou my flesh with thy fear" (Ps. 118:20). Bodily desires constitute the flesh, and the precepts of justice, the nails with which the fear of the Lord pierces our flesh and crucifies us as victims acceptable to the Lord. Whence the same Apostle says: "I exhort you, therefore, brethren, by the mercy of God, to present your bodies as a sacrifice, living, holy, pleasing to God." (Rom. 12:1)
>
> Hence, there is a cross in regard to which the servant of God, far from being confounded, rejoices, saying: "But as for me, God forbid that I should glory save in the cross of our Lord Jesus Christ, through whom the world is crucified to me, and I to the world" (Gal. 6:14). That is a cross, I say, not of forty days' duration, but of one's whole life. . . . Live always in this fashion, O Christian; if you do not wish to sink into the mire of this earth, do not come down from the cross.

The Response to Deogratias

In his response to the deacon of Carthage, Augustine set down his own understanding of religious education. He admitted to the difficulties of the task, and his own dissatisfaction with his efforts. But he not only outlined the method of narration which the catechist should follow. At the conclusion of the treatise he provided also a longer and a shorter example of a catechism. Both outlined the story of salvation and the work of Christ. In the briefer form of instruction Augustine described again, as he had so often before, the meaning of the death of Christ:

> As death entered into the human race by one man who was the first created, that is, Adam, because he consented to his wife, who had been led astray by the devil, so that they transgressed the commandment of God; so through one man who is also God, Jesus Christ, after their past sins had been utterly blotted out, all

who believe in him might enter into eternal life.

Once a flood took place over the whole earth, that sinners might be destroyed. And yet those who escaped in the Ark were a figure of the Church that was to be, which now floats upon the waves of the world, and is saved from sinking by the wood of the Cross of Christ.

It was foretold by the Prophets that he should suffer upon the Cross. . . . It was foretold that he should rise again. He rose again. And according to the very predictions of the Prophets, he ascended into heaven and sent the Holy Spirit to his disciples.

Do you, therefore, since you believe this, be on your guard against temptations (for the devil seeks some to perish with him), so that not only may that enemy fail to seduce you through those who are without the Church . . . but also that you may not imitate those in the Catholic Church herself whom you see leading evil lives, either those who indulge without restraint in the pleasures of the belly and the palate, or the unchaste, or those given to vain or unlawful practices, or of shows or of diabolical charms and divinations, or those who live in the pomp and vanity of covetousness and pride, or who lead any life that the Decalogue condemns and punishes; but may rather associate with the good, whom you will easily find, if you also are such yourself; so that together with them you may worship and love God for his own sake, for he himself shall be our whole reward, that we may have the fruition of his goodness and beauty in that blessed life. But he is to be loved not as anything that is seen by the eyes, but as wisdom is loved, and truth and holiness and justice and charity, and any other such virtues: not as these are found among men, but as they are in the very fount of incorruptible and unchangeable wisdom. Whomsoever therefore you see loving these virtues, to them be joined, that through Christ who became man that he might be the Mediator between God and man, you may be reconciled to God.

Imitate, then, the good, bear with the evil, love all; for you do not know what he shall be tomorrow who today is evil. And do not love their wrongdoing; but love them to the end that they may attain holiness; for not only is love of God enjoined upon us, but likewise love of neighbor, and on these two commandments depend the whole law and the prophets.

When Deogratias turned to his task of instructing the inquirers, he had an end to which he could refer all that he had to say. But still there were questions: Where in the Bible should he begin? What was essential in speaking about the faith? How should our salvation be explained? What should a catechism say?

BIBLIOGRAPHY

The following materials were used in the preparation of this case and are recommended for further study.

Bonner, G. *St. Augustine of Hippo: Life and Controversies.* The Westminster Press, 1963.

Burnaby, J. *Amor Dei: A Study of the Religion of St. Augustine.* London: Hodder & Stoughton, Ltd., 1938.

Campenhausen, Hans von. *The Fathers of the Latin Church.* Translated by Manfred Hoffman. Stanford University Press, 1969.

Frend, W. H. C. *The Donatist Church: A Movement of Protest in Roman North Africa.* Oxford: Clarendon Press, 1952.

Harnack, Adolf von. *History of Dogma,* Vol. V. Dover Publications, Inc., 1961.

Marrou, H. I. *St. Augustine and His Influence Through the Ages.* Translated by Patrick Hepburne-Scott. Harper & Brothers, Harper Torchbooks, 1957.

Nock, A. D. *Conversion: The Old and the New in Religion from Alexander the Great to Augustine of Hippo.* Oxford University Press, 1933.

O'Meara, J. *The Young Augustine, The Growth of Augustine's Mind Up to His Conversion.* Longmans, Green & Co., Inc., 1954.

Portalie, E. *A Guide to the Thought of St. Augustine.* Translated by Ralph J. Bastian. London: Burns, Oates & Washbourne, Ltd., 1960.

Van der Meer, Frederick. *Augustine the Bishop: The Life and Work of a Father of the Church.* Translated by Brian Buttershaw and G. R. Lamb. Sheed & Ward, Inc., 1962.

6
Abelard, Bernard,
and the Council of Sens
(A.D. 1140)

Peter Abelard knew that he was in the most difficult position of his life. He had suffered many adversities as a man, as a philosopher, and as a theologian. Now on Sunday, June 3, 1140, at the Council of Sens he faced an audience that included the king of France and many bishops from the area. On the day before, his chief accuser, Bernard of Clairvaux, had listed his heresies and asked prayer in his behalf. The accusations were many, but they centered on alleged misinterpretations of the nature of the atonement, and the relationship of faith and reason in Christian theology. Now Abelard considered whether to recant, compromise, or keep up the battle. He had to decide quickly how to respond.

Background: The Twelfth-Century Milieu

The early twelfth century in the world of Abelard and Bernard exhibited some of the most blatant shortcomings of the feudal age. Popes and kings struggled against each other with seemingly little permanent effect in an attempt to centralize power. National rulers were in constant warfare against regional lords and princes. Apparently no rule in the Western world could be universally acknowledged. Many robber barons, each a law to himself, pillaged the land. Popes also warred against rivals, and on at least six occasions during the years from 1100 to 1138 counterclaims to the papacy resulted in the branding of "antipopes." In much of the church there was corruption and disorder, with many abbots living in selfish luxury from

This case study was prepared by Professor Jack Rogers of Fuller Theological Seminary with the assistance of James Richardson. It is intended as a basis for class discussion rather than to illustrate either effective or ineffective handling of a situation.

money gathered from the poor by force. And nobles paid the church frequently in lieu of remonstration for their sins.

Into this confused situation two movements of reform brought the promise of progress and order—the one intellectual, the other experiential. An intellectual vitality arose from the study of Roman law and Greek philosophy. During this time a transformation occurred in the understanding of European law, and fresh winds of Aristotelianism fused life into the rather simplistic understanding of Platonism that had prevailed. Abelard, among others, revived interest in the science of "dialectic," and embryonic universities sprang up to replace cathedral schools as centers of scholarship.

The experiential movement centered on a thoroughgoing reform of monastic life. There arose a new piety yoked with a strong desire for subjective experience of redemption and illumination. Institutions for monastic living flourished, and new orders sprang up alongside the more established ones. Bernard exemplified this serious reorientation of the Christian life toward devotion and personal discipline.

In education, the authority of the Scriptures, of the Christian fathers, and of the church was not supplanted. But it was augmented by Aristotelianism, especially when new translations of Aristotle's work became available. The "seven liberal arts," which were thought to encompass all knowledge, remained standard fare for students: the trivium (grammar, rhetoric, and dialectic), and the quadrivium (arithmetic, geometry, music, and astronomy). Higher education throughout the eleventh century had been accomplished almost exclusively in the monastic schools which dotted the countryside. Of these, only Bec in Normandy remained significant through the twelfth century. General education had little place in the program of the order; and the monasteries were left in relative isolation, which suited their purposes. Within these institutions, the learning had been based on monastic ideas of apprenticeship—a master/learner emulation model of education.

As growing cities vied for independence the initiative in developing culture and education passed to their hands. Cathedral schools in Paris, Rheims, Tours, Laon, and Chartres became the foundation on which French universities developed. Paris in Abelard's time already occupied the *axis mundi* position as a center of learning, a place it would keep for centuries to come. Here more than anywhere else twelfth-century creative learning focused.

Background: Personalities Involved

Anselm of Canterbury

The first theologian of the period to use effectively a dialectical method for understanding God was Anselm of Canterbury (1033/34-1109). He proved to be not only a monk and a scholar but also a reformer and a church administrator of note. He entered the Abbey of Bec at the age of twenty-six, and after participating in its life for more than two decades was unanimously elected its abbot in 1078. Under his leadership, Bec gained renown in the realms of philosophical and theological studies. Anselm's published works drew laudatory comparison with those of the venerated Augustine. In 1093, Anselm was designated archbishop of Canterbury. He struggled throughout the remainder of his life to gain freedom for the church against the temporal power of successive English kings who controlled ecclesiastical appointments.

Anselm sought to prove the truths of faith both by meditating on analogies of Creation and Trinity (as Augustine had done), and by employing reason as a category for the theological enterprise. He naturally accepted faithfully the authority of the Scriptures and that of the church fathers. His intellectual pursuits were never divorced from his contemplative life as a monk. But, for Anselm, faith should lead to understanding. He perceived that faith should be an indispensable first step on the ladder of one's progression toward beatitude. Above faith would come insight into more truthful faith, still attainable on earth. Immediate experience of God's presence (the beatific vision) could come only after earthly life, a goal approached but never fully attained in the world. Thus he declared in his *Proslogion:*

> I do not seek, oh Lord, to penetrate your sublimity, as I can in no way compare my understanding to yours; but I do desire to understand in some fashion your truth, which my heart knows and loves. I mean I do not seek to understand so that I can believe, but rather believe that I might understand.

Although he read the fragments of Aristotle's work available to him, Anselm remained essentially a realist (from *res*, "thing") in the Platonic-Augustinian tradition. He therefore opposed the nominalism of Roscelin of Compiègne (d. ca. 1120), who contended that universals (abstract general principles) have no objective reference, but rather are only names. Anselm developed an ontological argument for the existence of God on the premise that he could think of a being than which nothing greater could be conceived. Since a being that really existed would be greater than one merely imagined, Anselm reasoned that God must necessarily exist. For if God existed in thought only, a yet greater being, existing in reality as well as in thought, could be conceived and the former would be a contradictory idea—a god that is not the greatest being.

Anselm's chief work, also his most widely read, was the dialogue on atonement, *Cur Deus homo (Why the God Man)*. In it he opposed the popular view that Christ in death repaid a debt owed to the devil, a mortgage payment that freed humanity from Satan's enslavement. He offered, rather, a "satisfaction," an "objective," or a "commercial" view that professed a debt owed—but one to God and not to the devil. Anselm likened God to a monarch who has been denied proper honor (a reflection in images of the medieval society in which he lived). Every sinner thus owes God satisfaction. Because God is infinite, only an infinite satisfaction would be appropriate. No one else, though, could make infinite satisfaction but God. And no one but a human being should make a human satisfaction on behalf of humanity. Thus for Anselm it was a logical necessity that God become human and die for the sins of human beings, rendering the satisfaction.

This work of Anselm helped to initiate a new theological era. He provided foundations for both the nascent scholastic and the monastic theologies that succeeded his. Anselm was a contemplative, though, whereas one of the principals at the coming Council of Sens was a professional scholar.

Peter Abelard

Born in Brittany in 1079, Abelard as a teen-ager declined the military career his father planned for him and became a self-described "peripatetic philosopher." He began from the age of fifteen to travel to any place where he could learn more of, or later teach, logic (or dialectic). His first teacher, Roscelin, proved to be a nominalist, and Abelard professed to have learned little from him. By way of contrast, his next master, William of Champeaux, the head of the Cathedral School of Notre Dame, was a realist in the mold of Anselm. Abelard, in testing his philosophical ability, challenged William to debate and defeated him from a middle-of-the-road, rather Socratic stance of questioning the master. William was evidently forced by Abelard's line of interrogation to modify his extremely Platonic position on the question of universals. Abelard's argument in this first fray was a "conceptualist" one—assuming that all human understanding arises from sensory experience but correlating that experience with the existent suprasensory world. Universals are not ultimately real, according to this way of thinking, but neither are they merely names of attributes or qualities. Thus, for the conceptualist, universals exist only in the mind; but they correspond to the reality which individuals have in common.

Abelard, never flagging in self-confidence during these early years, commented subsequently on his relationship to others in the school: "From the outset of my work in the school I began to gain such a name as a dialectician that the reputation of not only my fellow students but also of my teacher faded little by little." Buoyed by his large measure of self-appreciation, not to mention the accolades and stipends of some of his peers (in age only), Abelard established his own school in a suburb of Paris, and began teaching at the age of twenty-five. He also established a pattern (which was to be repeated) of attacking famous people and, by confronting them, gaining fame.

Alternating periods of teaching, retirement because of ill health, and turning to new horizons also characterized his further career. At the age of thirty-four, Abelard began the study of theology under the greatest academician in France, Anselm of Laon (1050–1117). Abelard soon found fault with his teacher's methods and proceeded to offer his own exegetical lectures on the Book of Ezekiel (some on one day's notice). "It was not my habit to make progress through diligence but through genius," he declared.

His success was so great that he earned the enmity of Anselm and the adulation of a number of the master's former students. Despite the efforts of both William of Champeaux and Anselm to prevent the appointment, Abelard was made master scholar at Notre Dame in Paris. Though now a church teacher, Abelard still was not required to be ordained, though ambition recommended him to be. Students flocked to him, and he acquired the wealth and fame to which he had aspired. And because of Abelard's efforts more than those of any other person, Paris developed into one of the real educational centers of the world—the locus of a first full university north of the Alps.

Abelard later reminisced that with success attained, he rapidly became quite bored facing a dearth of talented opponents. In his words:

Luck always makes fools conceited; worldly security slacks the power of the intellect and easily destroys it through the temptations of the flesh. I already considered myself the only philosopher left in the world, and no longer feared to be troubled by anyone. I then began to slacken the reins of lust, whereas I had previously lived outwardly continent.

Abelard fell in love with Heloise, the young niece of Fulbert, canon of Notre Dame. She was beautiful, brilliant, and cultured. So that he could be near her, he asked Fulbert if he might board in his home. Fulbert, eager to take advantage of the great scholar's presence, asked Abelard to attend to Heloise's education in his spare time. A passionate love affair followed. Abelard's students during 1117–1118 noticed the slackening of his scholarship. Very soon they knew the reason. Abelard had turned to writing love poems to Heloise and setting them to music. Students and common people were soon singing them. "All streets, every house, echoed with my name," Heloise later wrote. Finally Fulbert discovered the scandal and the lovers were parted. When Heloise learned that she was pregnant, Abelard abducted her and took her disguised as a nun to his sister's home in Brittany. There Heloise gave birth to a son they named Astrolabius. To mollify Fulbert, Abelard agreed to a *secret* marriage with Heloise so that he would not lose his teaching position. When Fulbert broadcast news of the marriage and mistreated Heloise for denying it, Abelard abducted her a second time and took her to a convent. Perhaps believing that Abelard was trying to get rid of Heloise, her uncle arranged a cruel punishment. Bribing Abelard's servant to open the door of his house by night, Fulbert's men took Abelard by surprise and castrated him. Overwhelmed with shame, Abelard entered the Benedictine monastery of St.-Denis to become a monk. At his command, Heloise first took religious orders and entered a convent.

Characteristically Abelard aroused the opposition of his fellow monks by offering proof that the monastery had not been founded by its supposed patron Dionysius the Areopagite. Soon he was back teaching in Paris. Abelard wrote a book for the use of his students, *On the Divine Unity and Trinity*. His method was clear:

> I . . . set out to develop the actual foundation of our belief by means of analogies taken from human reason. . . . Nothing could be believed unless it was first understood, and it was ridiculous for some to preach to others on matters neither they nor their listeners could understand.

The revolutionary nature of this method was perceived by Abelard's enemies. The Council of Soissons in 1121 condemned his teaching on the Trinity without giving him a chance to defend himself. He was forced to cast his book into the fire and was then shut up in his monastery. Abelard later reworked this book and published it as

Theologia Christiana. In it he introduced the word "theology" in the sense used since his time. The church fathers had never used it to refer to Christian doctrine, but only to what we call Greco-Roman mythology. Abelard never questioned the authority of the Scriptures or the church fathers. His concern was to interpret revelation in language and by analogies that humans could understand. Abelard had no desire to go beyond faith toward the beholding of God as did Anselm. He was content to try to understand. Dialectic was his way of defending the faith against false objections.

Perhaps because many in the church felt guilty about the illegal and unjust condemnation of Abelard at Soissons, he was permitted to leave the monastery of St.-Denis and again to teach. Abelard chose a remote spot near Troyes and about sixty miles from Clairvaux. There, on land given to him, he built a small chapel. He named it the Paraclete in memory of his "having come there as a fugitive" and in his despair "having found some repose in the consolations of divine grace." Even in that place the students found him and soon a school was flourishing. During the years from 1123 to 1126 a whole complex of buildings arose as more and more students came while Abelard wrote book after book.

Again Abelard's popularity caused his enemies to move against him. He was pressured into becoming abbot of the monastery of St.-Gildas-de-Ruys in faraway Brittany. It represented exile, and his life was endangered by the rough and immoral men, some even murderers, who had taken refuge behind a monk's cowl. In 1128 the nuns of the convent of Argenteuil were driven out with their prioress, Heloise, when a greedy abbot laid claim to their property. When Abelard learned this, he gave over to Heloise and her nuns his property, the Paraclete. In 1131 Pope Innocent II confirmed the deed of this gift to the nuns and their successors forever. For a time Abelard was happy visiting the nuns and acting as chaplain to them. When malignant rumors about his relationship to Heloise forced him to stay away, he and Heloise undertook an extensive correspondence. Heloise displayed her independence and brilliance in this situation, posing theological, liturgical, and ethical problems to Abelard. For his part, Abelard expressed his admiration and love for her now in the only way he could—by trying to help her live the life that he himself had decided upon for her. His recurrent theme was that her difficulties gave her an opportunity to gain a heavenly crown. He, on the other hand, was released from sensuality, but could expect no crown for it.

Abelard's view of the atonement may be related to his ethical theory. His central thesis can be traced to Heloise's letters reflecting upon their involvement: the goodness or wickedness of an act is dependent on intention alone. Applied to the atonement, it means that the decisive factor is the revelation of God's intention to love mankind. Abelard's view is called the "moral influence" or "subjective" theory. Christ's work, according to Abelard, consists in providing by teaching and example a manifestation of the love of God. That love is so great that it awakens in us an answering love.

> Our redemption is therefore this greatest love in us through Christ's suffering, the love which not only delivers us from the bondage of sin, but gains for us the true freedom of God's children, so that we, rather through love of Him than fear, fulfill all; He who has shown us such great mercy that none greater exists, as He himself witnessed: "Greater love, He says, hath no man than this, that a man lay down his life for his friends."

Abelard thereby rejected both the traditional theory that Christ had come to pay a debt to the devil and Anselm's theory that Christ had come to pay a debt to God.

Abelard had become a monk involuntarily. Yet now his "conversion" seemed complete. His philosophical and theological opinions did not change, but now they served a different purpose. After years of obscurity he reappeared in 1136 teaching in Paris.

Bernard of Clairvaux

One who seemed perfectly suited to living out the monastic ideal was Bernard of Clairvaux (1090–1153). Bernard distinguished himself both as a monastic recluse and as a church reformer whose influence touched all of Europe, including popes and kings. Bernard was of a noble family. At the age of twenty-one he determined, following the wishes of his dead mother, to enter a monastery. In 1112, taking four of his brothers and twenty-five friends with him, he presented himself at the Benedictine monastery in Cîteaux.

Since the development of the monastic rule by St. Benedict the rule had undergone some changes. The original three vows of chastity, poverty, and absolute obedience remained the foundation. Later, other rules were introduced. One was that the monk should remain in the house he had joined. Another divided the day into three parts—worship, manual labor, and study. A major alteration occurred when physical work in the fields was abandoned. At the time Bernard joined, most monasteries belonged to the congregation of Cluny, which had relaxed some of the extreme asceticism and concentrated on developing and performing an elaborate liturgy. At Cîteaux an attempt was being made to return to primitive simplicity. The Cistercian life was an active struggle to deny all physical enjoyment. Food was unflavored and kept at a minimum. Uncomfortable clothes and an uncomfortable bed were deliberately chosen. Prayer was limited to six hours a day and hard physical labor was reintroduced. Other physical and intellectual work was required. The Cistercian churches were absolutely plain. Anything that did not directly serve the end of mortification of the flesh was strictly forbidden. Study had no importance as such. The Bible and the church fathers were read as aids in the personal quest for holiness of life.

Bernard plunged wholeheartedly into this discipline and found ways of intensifying it for his personal development. He succeeded so well that after only three years he was chosen as abbot of a new house. With twelve companions he selected as the site a solitary valley called Clairvaux. He was ordained by William of Champeaux, now bishop of Châlons-sur-Marne. Thus, in 1115 at the age of twenty-five, he had attained a significant position of ecclesiastical leadership. When Bernard joined the Cistercian Order, it was small in number of priests; it was poor and had only two houses. The day when Bernard came with twenty-nine friends marked a new beginning for the order. At the end of Bernard's life the Cistercians numbered about seven hundred monks and lay brothers; they were immensely wealthy and had spread sixty-eight new houses throughout Europe. This growth was directly attributable to Bernard's preaching and his zeal for "converting" clerics, laymen, and monks from other orders. (Conversion was indicated by leaving a life in the world for that of the cloister.)

Bernard's single-minded dedication to the "evangelical perfection" of the monastic ideal led him freely to criticize others. He chastized other orders, particularly the congregation of Cluny under the leadership of Peter the Venerable, for their comparative laxity. Bernard participated in the reformation of other monastic orders and urged upon the parish clergy a communal and austere life-style similar to monastic life. These activities brought Bernard into church politics on a very large scale. He exercised significant influence over Count Theobald of Champagne in whose district Clairvaux lay. And Bernard did not hesitate to write instructions to the king of France and to the pope. From 1130 onward, Bernard was a political influence on a European scale. When the college of cardinals elected two rival popes, Bernard threw his influence behind Innocent II, who was forced to flee to France from his Italian rival Anacletus II. When Innocent II was finally triumphant in 1138, Bernard received much of the credit.

In Bernard's view, none of these activities were contrary to his concentration on personal religion. For him, it was the solitary life of prayer and meditation which made him aware of and able to exert the full claims of religion on the world. He seemed unable to consider the legitimacy of other points of view. His concerns were those of Christ and the church and he fought for them. He had almost no knowledge of the philosophers Plato and Aristotle. To him, they were mere sophists whose influence on education was bound to be harmful. Bernard was thoroughly conservative and traditional. The Scriptures and the church fathers were to be studied and repeated. He preferred to express himself in Biblical terms and found new theological ideas abhorrent. His literary activity was primarily in devotional works, especially a famous series of sermons on The Song of Songs, which he thoroughly allegorized.

The monastic theology of Bernard was not concerned with knowledge, but with love. The purpose of knowing God is that we might know ourselves as sinners and turn our wills to the total love of God which is our true purpose. The image of God in man is not reason, but free will. The monastic life was designed to kill self-will so that in true freedom we might be totally obedient to God. The means to this end are meditation on the life of Christ and on the sufferings of Mary for our sakes. Through continuous mortification and meditation, mystical experience develops. The language used to describe this movement toward full unity with the will of God is the language of marriage. It begins with "the bridegroom's visit." The final stage of rapturous, ecstatic experience of union with God is called "the bridegroom's kiss." A twelfth-century tradition tells that Bernard once was reciting the Ave Maria before a statue of the Virgin. When he came to the words, *"Monstra te esse Matrem,"* the image, pressing her breast, let fall on the lips of Bernard three drops of milk which had nourished the Savior.

Bernard's doctrine of the atonement combined several traditional theories. The human life and passion of Christ do not merely reveal the love of God, but effect it savingly. Thus, with Irenaeus and Athanasius, the incarnation is the saving entrance of God into humanity. Bernard uncritically accepted Gregory's notion that the devil has a just power over men because of our sin. Christ's death is a satisfaction of his debt to the devil. Although Bernard also had subjective elements in his view of the atonement, over against Abelard he strongly maintained the objective side:

That He gave to men by living and teaching an example of life; whilst by suffering and dying He set before us the extreme limit of charity. Did He therefore teach righteousness, and not give it; did He manifest charity, but not infuse it; and did He on these terms return to His own concerns?

To these elements, Bernard added a significant place for Mary in the work of redemption. Mary's mediation on our behalf was one of his favorite themes.

Bernard's monastic theology and mystical experience, aided by the miracles attributed to him, had profound influence on the doctrine and spirituality of the church. The Franciscan school which followed one hundred years later received its basic orientation from Bernard. The author of *The Imitation of Christ*, and other mystical writers, evidence being nourished by Bernard's writings.

Events Leading to the Council of Sens

Peter Abelard must have been very happy to resume teaching in Paris in 1136. The years of adversity and sorrow must have seemed finally behind him as students once again flocked to his lectures and his books were read everywhere. Once again, however, his popularity was to be his undoing.

A copy of Abelard's *Theologia* came into the possession of William of St. Thierry, at the Cistercian monastery of Signy. William may have been a fellow student with Abelard under Anselm of Laon in 1112 or 1113. Now, William's closest friend was Bernard of Clairvaux. Horrified at the contents of Abelard's book, William wrote to Bernard early in 1139. He also sent a copy to Geoffrey of Chartres, the papal legate in France, also a friend of Bernard. This same Geoffrey earlier had tried in vain to save Abelard from his unjust conviction at the Council of Soissons in 1121. William apparently believed that Abelard would fear these two men and might be dissuaded from his opinions by them. William's charges were clear:

Peter Abelard seized the moment, when all the masters of ecclesiastical doctrine have disappeared from the scene of the world, to conquer a place apart, for himself, in the schools, and to create there an exclusive domination. He treats Holy Scripture as though it were dialectics. It is a matter with him of personal invention and annual novelties. He is the censor and not the disciple of the faith; the corrector and not the imitator of the authorized masters.

Bernard acknowledged the seriousness of the matter in his reply and explained that his unfamiliarity with the matter was due to having been for some years in Italy working in support of Pope Innocent II. A meeting was arranged between William and Bernard just after Easter in 1139. Bernard left convinced that he must intervene against Abelard.

Bernard approached the archbishop of Sens, in whose ecclesiastical province Paris was, hoping that he would censure Abelard. When that came to nothing, Bernard wrote to the bishop of Paris, Abelard's superior. The bishop refused to intervene, but gave Bernard permission to preach in Paris. Bernard took this opportunity to make a sharp attack on Abelard with the hope of taking Abelard's students away from him. Undoubtedly this confrontation roused Abelard's anger.

Abelard and Bernard had probably known of each other for some time. They had surely met in 1131 at Morigni in the presence of Innocent II. Abelard had gone to ask that a papal legate come to reform the monastery of which he was abbot. Bernard was part of Innocent's retinue. Another involvement of Bernard and Abelard concerned the Paraclete, over which Heloise was then presiding as abbess. Heloise had invited Bernard to the convent perhaps to convince him that everything was going according to rule. Bernard was satisfied (and Heloise pronounced him an "angel") except for one detail in the liturgy. It happened that Abelard was the originator of the liturgical innovation and he wrote a spirited defense of it to Bernard.

A letter to the pope in the name of the bishops of France asserted that Bernard had initially cautioned Abelard secretly, then in the presence of two or three witnesses, all in a spirit of friendliness. Abelard clearly did not feel any friendliness from Bernard. He viewed Bernard's enmity as simply another case of envy on the part of someone intellectually inferior to himself.

Abelard then took the initiative. He appealed to the archbishop of Sens to allow him to defend his works publicly against Bernard. Since the archbishop had also been the subject of sharp criticism by Bernard, he willingly assumed the role of referee in a debate Abelard was sure to win. The date was set for Sunday, June 3, 1140. The date was chosen to assure a sizable and influential audience. On the Sunday after Whitsun, there was to be a great festival at Sens. The king and his court as well as bishops and abbots were expected to be present to view a display of relics at Sens cathedral.

Bernard was not pleased with this turn of events. He later explained in a letter to the pope the reasons for his reluctance to engage in debate:

When all fly before him he challenges me, the weakest of all to single combat. The Archbishop of Sens, at his request, writes to me fixing a day. . . . I refused, not only because I am a youth and he an experienced warrior, but also because I thought it unfitting that the grounds of faith should be discussed by human reasoning when it is agreed that it rests on such a firm and sure foundation.

At length, Bernard's friends persuaded him to confront Abelard for fear that if Bernard defaulted, Abelard's reputation would become even greater.

Both sides gathered their forces for the debate in an atmosphere of suspicion and hostility. Abelard wrote to his friends pleading his cause as a scholar who had been impugned. For him it was to be a matter of academic argument. He had no doubt as to who would win. Bernard wrote to the bishops. He pled not his own cause, but that of Christ and the church. The issue as he put it was not an academic one, but a holy war against heresy. Bernard cast himself as the personification of the church. Abelard he characterized as the embodiment of evil powers opposing God.

The crowd gathered in a holiday mood. On the morning of June 2, 1140, Bernard preached to the people of Sens and stirred them up against Abelard while asking them to pray for him. Later in the day Bernard assembled the six bishops for a consultation. They had been well prepared by Bernard through correspondence. One of them was a relative and fellow monk of Bernard's. One of Abelard's friends contended that the consultation was held after dinner. The bishops had drunk quite a bit of wine and were very sleepy. And Abelard's writings were hard reading. Bernard produced a list of propositions that he attributed to Abelard. Many of them bore little resemblance to Abelard's views. Some that did express his teaching included:

4. That Christ did not take the flesh in order to free us from the yoke of the Devil.
6. That free will of itself suffices to do some good.
9. That we have not received the guilt of Adam, but only the penalty.
10. That those who crucified Christ did not sin, for they did not know what they were doing, and that there is no guilt in that which is done out of ignorance.
12. That the power to bind and unbind was given only to the apostles, and not to their successors.

Bernard then pressed the bishops to condemn Abelard's teaching. One reporter contended that it was difficult for the sleepy prelates to pronounce *damnamus* ("we condemn"). They dropped the first syllable, and saying *namus* ("we are floating") they betrayed their sodden condition. Bernard had accomplished his goal. The judgment was certain in advance.

Abelard got word of the bishops' proceedings. His hope of a free debate before an impartial audience was shattered. He had come willing to be corrected if shown that he had written contrary to the Catholic faith. His attitude was "Strike, but hear me." Now he knew that he would not be heard, but would be condemned. He would have no opportunity to defend his views of the nature of the atonement and the relationship of faith and reason in Christian theology. So, he carefully considered what he should do under these new circumstances. Must he recant? Was a compromise possible? Could he in some way carry on his fight to be vindicated?

The next day, on June 3, 1140, Abelard entered the cathedral at Sens. A great assembly headed by the king and the bishops was awaiting him. By prior arrangement with the bishops, Bernard read aloud a list of propositions. He concluded with the pronouncement that Abelard could now admit or deny authorship and then either renounce or defend his ideas. Abelard looked at the crowd. What should he do?

BIBLIOGRAPHY

The following materials were used in the preparation of this case and are recommended for further study.

Adams, Henry. *Mont-Saint-Michel and Chartres.* Houghton Mifflin Company, 1936.

Ferm, Robert L. *Readings in the History of Christian Thought.* Holt, Rinehart & Winston, Inc., 1964.

Franks, Robert S. *The Work of Christ: A Historical Study of Christian Doctrine.* Thomas Nelson & Sons, 1962.

Grane, Leif. *Peter Abelard: Philosophy and Christianity in the Middle Ages.* Translated by Frederick and Christine Crowley. Harcourt, Brace Jovanovich, Inc., 1970.

Murray, A. Victor. *Abelard and St. Bernard: A Study in Twelfth Century "Modernism."* Barnes & Noble, Inc., 1967.

7

Luther, Carlstadt,

and Protestant Reform (A.D. 1521)

Exiled in the Wartburg Castle during the winter of 1521–22, Martin Luther received news from Wittenberg that reform actions were being instigated there in abundance. Communion was being given in both kinds. The hermits of St. Anthony, on one of their normal rounds as mendicants, had been bombarded with muck by university students. Luther's fellow Augustinians, and the Franciscans too, were leaving the orders in droves. People stopped coming to confession. And right before Christmas, Andrew Bodenstein of Carlstadt announced that he himself would serve the laity in both kinds, actually letting them take the elements from the altar themselves. He would employ an abbreviated service, and he would wear the clothes of the people instead of clerical vestments. When the members of the town council and the Elector Frederick objected to Carlstadt's intentions, Carlstadt pre-empted their denial of his actions by proceeding quickly to do what he had promised—and on Christmas Day.

Despite the fact that Carlstadt several times was the respondent to calls for reform from university students, townspeople, and colleagues, and seldom the initiator, he did represent for Luther an epitome of the problem—how to implement Scriptural teaching about grace, law, redemption, and Christian life. Luther felt strongly that many church practices mistook magic and church superstitions as substitutes for essential faith in Jesus Christ. But should not the people learn to walk in reforming their religious practice before they commenced running? Just how far should Christian iconoclasm go in severing Christian community from its heritage and traditions? Specifically, how should he respond to the situation in Wittenberg?

This case study was prepared by Professor Louis Weeks of the Louisville Presbyterian Theological Seminary as a basis for class discussion rather than to illustrate either effective or ineffective handling of a situation.

Martin Luther

Luther was raised in a moderately prosperous family and received a standard liberal arts education at Erfurt in preparation for the study of law. After being awarded an M.A. in 1505, however, Luther turned instead to a religious life in the Augustinian monastery in that city. In doing so, he fulfilled a personal vow, taken in desperation in the midst of a summer thunderstorm. He likewise disappointed his father, Hans, who nevertheless was later reconciled to Luther's new vocational commitment. The young priest celebrated his first Mass in 1507, and he moved quickly to a position of responsibility within the order as subprior of the Wittenberg monastery (1511) and as vicar of the district (1515). He also was awarded a doctorate in theology in 1512 and proceeded to lecture at Wittenberg's infant university on Psalms, Romans, Galatians, and Hebrews.

Luther became increasingly convinced that Christian salvation was not a matter of people meriting anything, but rather that it remained a divine action of "grace alone," given through Jesus Christ. He apprenticed himself to the writings of Augustine and other church fathers as well as to the actual books of Scripture. He discerned that the sacramental and monastic systems of offering to people avenues of becoming "true and perfect Christians" through the grace mediated by the church had frequently turned into impediments to the full reception of the meaning of Jesus' cross and resurrection in the life of faith. In his own life, Luther determined that the more he confessed his sin, a prerequisite to Christian growth in grace, the more he needed to confess. Liberation for him personally occurred in his experiencing the valuelessness of works and the forgiveness God gave in faith. Christian righteousness, Luther came to see, was purely a gift, for which no one could prepare and from which any person (lay or clergy) could know God's grace in relation with Jesus Christ.

In a letter to George Spalatin, liaison between Luther and the court of the Elector Frederick, Luther described his feelings about the law and criticized even the noted Erasmus of Rotterdam for overestimating human ability. "The 'righteousness based upon the law' or 'upon deed' is, therefore, in no way merely a matter of (religious) ceremonial but rather of the fulfillment of the entire Decalogue. Fulfillment without faith in Christ . . . no more resembles righteousness than sour apples resemble figs." Rather, the righteous person produces good actions, and the first requisite is that a person "be changed" by God. "Abel pleases [God] before his gift does."

Already convinced of the necessity of undoing church abuses of Scriptural Christianity, Luther became incensed at the blatant commercialism and false theology involved in the papal sale of jubilee indulgences for the building of St. Peter's basilica in Rome. Commissioned first by Pope Julius II in 1510, the sale of penitential favors was revived in 1515 in the reign of Leo X. John Tetzel, subcommissioner under Albrecht, the bishop of Mainz, was advertising release for a beneficiary of one's choice from purgatory in direct exchange for monies received. This double travesty—the mechanization of the already questionable practice of granting private confession as a way of aiding the salvation process—prompted Luther to offer in print a list of Ninety-five Theses, or "Disputation of the Power and Efficacy of Indulgences." He called into question both the theory and the practice of current indulgence selling. Penance should be a way of life, and not a sneaky way for the wealthy to receive salvation.

The Theses attracted immediate and wide public attention, and the Roman authorities began at once to investigate areas in which Luther's statements might be heretical. Luther, protected by the confused political milieu in Germany and by the direct support of the Elector Frederick of Saxony, survived the first onslaught of investigations. His opponents, who not only believed in the sacramental efficacy of penance but also reckoned practically that the money gained from the sale of indulgences would be necessary for the maintenance of the church, settled temporarily for an academic disputation instead of an outright heresy trial. Thus the Leipzig Disputation matched John Eck of Ingolstadt, champion of the Catholic forces, against Luther and his senior colleague, Carlstadt.

Andrew Bodenstein of Carlstadt, and the Wittenberg Movement

Born about 1477 in Franconia, Carlstadt studied at both Erfurt and Cologne before being called to Wittenberg in 1505. There he began teaching and writing, mostly Thomistic philosophy. Parlaying a leave of absence into a major sabbatical and a law degree, he returned to the young university full of vigor and with his world view in flux. He steeped himself in the studies of Augustinian theology as a result of a debate with Luther in 1516, and less than a year later published a compilation of theses on "Grace." A commentary on a tract by Augustine, *The Spirit and the Letter,* followed soon after. In it Carlstadt argued that God's grace is everywhere apparent in the Christian life. The idea of people producing any merit, even secondarily causing their own initiation into the ranks of the redeemed, he ridiculed as absurd. Both congruent and condignant merit he held to be untenable. Thus God is known by revelation—not by any system of earning anything. This point of view placed Carlstadt, by now dean of the Wittenberg faculty, alongside Luther. He published a list of Theses supporting Luther, defending the primacy of Biblical authority, and justifying the changes undertaken in the Wittenberg curriculum as a result of their "new" theology.

The challenge to defend the "new doctrines" was actually presented to Carlstadt, with Luther's name only an addendum. This may well have been a deliberate snub of Luther, a bow to academic protocol and Carlstadt's rank, or an honest opinion of the authorities that Carlstadt was "in charge" of the movement.

By now, however, Luther evidently was the polemical and theological head of a growing body of dissenting church people. In addition to Carlstadt, they had also the services of Philip Melanchthon, Gabriel Zwilling, Justus Jonas, and others. Melanchthon, Luther's closest companion, proved a learned and moderate contributor to the new theological milieu.

Zwilling, an Augustinian monk, was a fiery preacher and iconoclast. Jonas, provost of the All Saints Church and a faculty member of the university, had administrative skills and preaching ability too.

The Leipzig Events

John Eck chose Leipzig as the place for the disputation to be held rather than Erfurt, where Luther and Carlstadt could muster greater support. In June, 1519, when the Wittenberg contingent was entering the city, Carlstadt's wagon had a wreck and Carlstadt fell unceremoniously into the street. He injured himself, and physicians bled him as a curative measure. He therefore was scarcely at his best for the debate.

John Eck also chose to focus his attack primarily on the theology as Luther espoused it. Eck treated the arguments made by Carlstadt with an air of benign neglect. He did, however, concede to Carlstadt (perhaps as a stratagem) the primary place in the debate as opponent, so the Eck/Luther exchanges proved to be a kind of half-time show in the midst of the Eck/Carlstadt engagement. The latter, nevertheless, turned out to be deadly boring for most of the audience, focusing on such trivialities as whether God had created a work "good" wholly, but not entirely. Such distinctions—and there were others of equal "severity"—paled before the serious grappling of Luther and Eck with the question of papal primacy. Luther had hoped to center on the obvious Biblical insistence on grace over free will (and the *Freedom of a Christian Man* later reflected his point of view). But

Luther was willing courageously to doubt the primacy of all authority save Scripture itself. Yes, there was a definite need for a pope as interpreter and guide of the church; but there was little Scriptural justification of apostolic succession by the Vicar of Rome and still less for any qualitative distinction between the pope and other Christians. Christ was, and remains, the founder and primate of the church. Eck conceded that the indulgence system proved neither Scriptural nor necessary, but he retained the right of the pope to grant pardon from purgatory. Luther, for his part, granted the possibility of Scriptural references to a purgatory, and claimed that if the curia held Eck's position of the subject, there would be no need for the present disputation. Eck asserted that Luther was following in the footsteps of John Hus, the Czech heretic, and Luther admitted that certain doctrines of Hus had some merit.

After Luther and Eck contested, Carlstadt returned to battle Eck some more. But the theologically unsophisticated members of the audience tired of this "third round," and the whole disputation on dogma and papal prerogatives just petered out. The Wittenbergers returned home, and Eck reported to Rome that he had vanquished the "Hussites." Carlstadt, as full of vitriol as Eck, published an assessment of the papal champion entitled *Against the Dumb Ass and Stupid Little Doctor.*

The Diet of Worms, and Afterward

On July 15, 1520, the pope promulgated *Exsurge, Domini,* a bull of particulars condemning Luther's theology *in toto.* Eck, taking the bull northward to publish it in Germany, added Carlstadt's name also among others whose works were declared heretical. Luther's works underwent a public burning, and their author was admonished to repent and retract his erroneous views. German communities refused to post the bull. Luther, in his own bonfire consisting of works by Eck and some volumes of canon law, threw in a copy of the pope's document for good measure.

For a trial on these charges of heresy, a Diet was summoned at Worms. In a series of complicated procedures extending in time from January to mid-April of 1521, the judging of Luther's orthodoxy continued. Luther himself appeared, on the promise of safe-conduct, and spoke eloquently in defense of his position. Some of his works Luther would be willing to repudiate—those which the Diet could show in error by appeal to the Scriptures. In the final analysis, though, he would not recant anything, "for to go against conscience is neither right nor safe." "God help me," he implored. Relieved after giving his "simple answer," Luther also provoked the emperor to condemn him.

The Edict of Worms, signed by the emperor on the twenty-sixth of May after a period of delay, accused Luther of making the efficacy of the sacraments depend on the faith of the recipient and of inciting the peasants to revolt; and it ordered the eradication of his works and his seizure as a heretic. Nevertheless Luther's safe-conduct to Worms had been honored; and on his way back to Wittenberg, Luther was kidnapped. In fact, he took up residence in the Wartburg, protected again by the Elector of Saxony.

In the Wartburg, Luther worked feverishly on his writings—expositions of the psalms, encouragements to colleagues, devotional writings, and Biblical translation. But he could not avoid hearing of the implementation of reform in Wittenberg.

During the summer months of 1521, Carlstadt went to Denmark at the invitation of the king, Christian II, and spent about six weeks consulting on the implementation of reform there. He returned to Wittenberg, though, and proceeded to rejoin efforts at home. The movement seemed at this point rather stymied from two directions —on the one hand townspeople were expressing some distrust in the eradication of objects of devotion and instrumentalities for performing acts of pietism; on the other hand, the elector himself at times seemed to threaten reformers with his conservatism. He had ordered the town council to punish anyone who destroyed religious objects, or interrupted devotional activity, or in other ways became a "public nuisance." The council should approve unanimously reforms in advance of their institution, especially in the observance of the Mass.

It was in this context that Justus Jonas preached a provocative diatribe against indulgences, private Masses, and vigils. Melanchthon began to offer both elements to communicants. And Carlstadt truncated the Mass itself on Christmas Day. Zwilling also moved into active reform, agitating for the renunciation of Augustinian vows by the Wittenberg chapter of friars. Luther confirmed for himself the knowledge of the problems in a secret visit to the city in December.

The beginnings of really radical alterations in religious observance were being encouraged early in 1522 by a group of "prophets" who came to Wittenberg and caught the attention of both Carlstadt and Melanchthon. Marcus Stübner, a former student at the university and a friend of Melanchthon, Nicholas Storch, a weaver and student of the Bible, and Thomas Drechsel were all disciples of Thomas Münzer. Münzer and the "prophets" had been recently expelled from the Saxon village of Zwickau for being a public nuisance.

Frederick, and Luther too, considered these Anabaptists to be religious anarchists. The prophets believed in the literal following of Scriptural admonitions from the Old as well as the New Testament. Cardinal among their theological commitments was a belief in "believer's baptism." Infants should not be received into a baptized communion, because the Bible showed that Jesus received the sacrament as an adult. Likewise the early church practiced adult baptism. Salvation came, according to these prophets, by God's supernatural action. Many such persons also prayed and believed that Jesus would return in short order to claim righteous followers and begin the earthly reign.

Melanchthon and Carlstadt listened to the men and were impressed by their knowledge of the Bible. By the end of January, the city council had approved the changes already made—it ordered the removal of altars in most churches, communion in both kinds, and new fiscal measures to care for the poor but to end mendicant activity.

According to most sources, Zwilling more than Carlstadt was leading the townspeople to destroy pictures of saints, smash their images, and throw out altars. But Carlstadt's leadership was apparent in his acquiescence. Carlstadt even sought to abolish organs and trumpets from the churches.

Melanchthon wrote to Luther asking about the extent to which the church should follow Carlstadt, Zwilling, and the Zwickau prophets. Luther had specific ideas about the prophets, and he immediately penned a response to Melanchthon's inquiry.

"Spirits are to be tested. If you cannot test them, then you have the advice of Gamaliel that you postpone judgment. . . . I do not want the 'prophets' to be accepted if they state that they were called by mere revelation."

Luther also disapproved that they taught only believer's baptism, but mainly he feared their influence in accelerating the reform measures at a time when consolidation of gains already made should occupy the church.

Carlstadt was urging more reforms, and published a pamphlet, "Of the putting away of Pictures, and that there should be no beggars among Christians in the Christian City of Wittenberg." He was taking seriously the law of the Old Testament, applying in the Christian context univocally the commands of God for the pre-Christian community, as Luther interpreted it. And perhaps Luther also was jealous of Carlstadt's leading the church in reform.

The Decision

Invitations were coming for Luther to return to Wittenberg. Should he go back, seek to move again the reform according to his own designs? Would he violate the relative political peace by reentering the public arena?

Feeling desperation at the Wittenberg situation, Luther considered his possible courses of action. Return would mean increased chances that he would pay bodily for his deviance from orthodoxy. Staying would mean that reform would be more rapid than he desired. If he did go back to Wittenberg, what actions should he take to reseize the reins of the reform movement? How could Scriptural teachings about grace, law, redemption, and the Christian life be implemented without causing disorder in the Christian community?

BIBLIOGRAPHY

The following materials were used in the preparation of this case and are recommended for further study.

Chadwick, Owen. *The Reformation.* Wm. B. Eerdmans Publishing Company, 1964.

Green, V. H. H. *Luther and the Reformation.* London: B. T. Batsford, Ltd., 1964.

Grimm, Harold J. *The Reformation Era.* The Macmillan Company, 1954, 1973.

Hillerbrand, Hans Joachim. *The Reformation.* Harper & Row, Publishers, Inc., 1964.

Lortz, Joseph. *The Reformation.* Translated by John C. Dwyer, S.J. The Newman Press, 1964.

Rupp, Gordon. *Luther's Progress to the Diet of Worms.* Harper & Brothers, 1951.

———. *Patterns of Reformation.* London: The Epworth Press, 1969.

8

Calvin and the Italian Anti-Trinitarians (A.D. 1558)

Giovanni Valenti Gentile had one chance to escape death. He had come from his native Italy to Geneva in 1556 attracted by the reputation of Calvin. Now, only two years later, he was condemned to death by the Genevan Council. His only hope for mercy was to perform a humiliating act of penance. He would have to kneel barefoot before his judges, clad only in a shirt and carrying a torch, and beg God and them for mercy and then burn all his writings. Should he do it? The immediate choice for him was life or death. But for others the issues that had precipitated the crisis would remain: Could there be civil tolerance of religious differences? What was the truth of the doctrine of the Trinity? What rights did lay people have to develop theology over against the professional theologians of the church? Gentile knew that his choice affected many. And he did not have long to decide.

Calvin in Geneva

As a city, Geneva had been experimenting with reform even before the coming of Calvin. But the Council had joined belatedly with Guillaume Farel in inviting the young French immigrant to help out in 1536. Calvin, then at the age of twenty-seven, had already become converted from the Catholicism of his youth and now sought to implement Biblical Christianity as Luther and the humanists interpreted it. A scant year and a half later the Reformers were likewise invited (under penalty of incarceration if they refused) to leave the

This case study was prepared by Professor Jack Rogers of Fuller Theological Seminary with the assistance of James Richardson. It is intended as a basis for class discussion rather than to illustrate either effective or ineffective handling of a situation.

city. They had consistently "mixed themselves in magistracy," interfered with city politics in behalf of the gospel they proclaimed. Calvin, sojourning in Strasbourg, where he married and also ministered to refugees, continued to be popular with some of Geneva's factions. With another change in power, he returned and undertook permanent residence in 1541. The city's factionalism continued, though, and it was not until 1555 with the expulsion of the Perrinists that John Calvin's party could finally implement its theology of culture.

Calvin's *Institutes of the Christian Religion* in various editions systematically set forth Protestant principles (although the work never represented Protestant consensus on those theological tenets). Calvin himself envisioned a Christ-centered community on earth. It would not culturally attain any hint of the divine Kingdom of God to come. Civil law would serve to contain the human (fallen) propensity for self-destruction. Salvation, given freely in God's own time to those whom God chose, remained unmerited in any respect, as it had been for Luther. Calvin considered Biblical and patristic doctrines (formulations and creeds by the early church) basic to Christian life —belief in the authority of Scripture, the Trinity, symbols pertaining to the nature of Christ, and the Catholicity of the church among them. Thus, at the height of his municipal power in 1556, Calvin sought to foment Christian revolution in behalf of reformation in Roman territories; but he was never willing to broach dissenting theologies that might undermine the things already achieved.

Italian Refugee Radicals—Forerunners of Unitarianism

Italians who rejected the dogmas of the Roman Catholic Church were compelled to flee Italy in the face of the Inquisition. Most of these Italian refugees were attracted to the liberating teachings of the Swiss Reformers in Zurich and Geneva. In 1542 an Italian Protestant congregation was formed in Geneva under Bernardino Ochino (1487–1564). Ochino had been a leader among strict Franciscan monks. Contact with Peter Martyr Vermigli had persuaded him to accept Protestant doctrines. Ochino did not stay long in Geneva, whence he had fled from the Inquisition. He soon accepted an invitation from Thomas Cranmer to go to England. By 1555 he was back in Switzerland as pastor of the Italian congregation in Zurich. He was expelled from this office in 1563 for his views on the Trinity and monogamy. He then went to Poland and for a brief period took part in the reform movement there.

The Italian congregation in Geneva lay dormant from the time of

Ochino's pastorate until 1552, when it was reorganized as a church under the Genevan model. Sunday services, weekday Bible studies, and theological discussions were held. During this time the congregation grew in size and enthusiasm. Calvin tolerated the Italian Protestants, but considered their doctrine and discipline rather wayward. He became increasingly uneasy about their theological discussions. This was partly because he was not able to monitor them, since they were conducted in Italian.

Most of the Italian refugees were people of the second generation of the Reformation. Most were well educated. They shared sentiments of skepticism with the people of the Renaissance, of humanism with Erasmus, and of radicalism with the Anabaptists. Not one of the influential Italian Protestants had been trained as a theologian.

The Servetus Affair

An additional factor that united the Italians was their response to the fate of another refugee in Geneva, Michael Servetus (1511–1553). Servetus was a Spanish humanist who was thoroughly educated in Biblical languages, law, and medicine. He had imbibed the religious skepticism of late fifteenth-century Italy. On the basis of his Biblical studies, in 1531, when he was barely twenty, he published a treatise entitled *On the Errors of the Trinity*. Servetus' doctrine was a form of Sabellian modalism. Father, Son, and Holy Spirit were simply three "modes" or manifestations of God. Jesus was considered divine, but not in the orthodox sense.

Servetus' treatise shocked his Protestant friends. He proceeded to Paris to study medicine and was a practicing physician there from 1541 to 1553. During this time he entered into correspondence with Calvin, who repudiated Servetus' anti-Trinitarian views.

In 1553 Servetus' principal work appeared: *Christianismi restitutio*. In it he denied both the Trinity and the divinity of Christ. This book was denounced by the Catholic Inquisition, and Servetus was imprisoned for heresy. He managed to escape to Geneva, possibly counting on help from the anti-Calvinists. Calvin had him arrested, and when he refused to recant, he was burned at the stake as a heretic on October 27, 1553. As the flames tortured him, he was heard to cry: "O God, save my soul; O Jesus, Son of the eternal God, have mercy on me." An onlooker is reported to have remarked that if Servetus had placed the adjective "eternal" before "Son," he would have been allowed to live.

Leaders of the Italian Protestants in Geneva

Matthew Gribaldi (1506–1564)

Gribaldi was one of the most famous jurists of his time. In 1541 he published a well-known textbook on civil law. He taught law in some ten different universities in France, Italy, and Germany. He was a rationalistic humanist who was sympathetic to the Reformation. Gribaldi married a Frenchwoman who had an estate at Farges, about twenty miles west of Geneva. They spent nearly every summer at Farges. Gribaldi took great interest in the trial of Servetus and, in September, wrote a letter about it to the "brethren of Vicenza," a group of radicals with an anti-Trinitarian and anabaptist reputation.

At the end of his vacation, Gribaldi passed through Geneva on his way back to the university in Padua, where he taught. Being a famous professor of civil law, Gribaldi was asked while in Geneva what his views were on the proceedings against Servetus. Gribaldi expressed his opinion that no one should be put to death for his religious views, no matter how heretical they seemed. Unwillingly, Gribaldi was forced into a discussion of the unity of God in which he expressed agreement with Servetus' views. Offense was taken to this in Geneva. Gribaldi then proposed that the issue be discussed openly and invited Calvin to join in the debate. Calvin refused. Gribaldi was greatly disturbed by what he considered Calvin's haughtiness and left the city. On his way through Zurich, Gribaldi bitterly complained to Bullinger about his treatment at Geneva. After Servetus' execution, in the winter of 1553, Gribaldi was given a copy of Servetus' *De Trinitatis erroribus.* He later confessed that reading it brought him to know Christ.

In the autumn of the following year while in Geneva, Gribaldi was again dragged into a discussion of the doctrine of the Trinity. He rejected orthodox explanations and asserted that he could find a better explanation which would harmonize with both reason and Scripture. Later in 1554, he was again in Geneva and was summoned by Calvin before the church council for examination. When Calvin refused to shake hands with him at this meeting, Gribaldi left in anger. Since he was a foreigner and not likely to be converted anyway, the Council members decided not to take any further action. Gribaldi again complained to Bullinger at Zurich, but Bullinger sternly cautioned him against spreading heresy. Feeling that he might be in danger, Gribaldi volunteered to write a confession in which he professed the orthodox doctrine.

Gribaldi's theological views were simplistic and bordered on tritheism. In a later work, *De vera cognitione Dei*, Gribaldi declared that the three persons of the Trinity were three distinct Gods, but that "God the highest is like Jove, the first among them." He actually held a ditheism, since he neglected to deal with the third Person. It was blasphemous to begin with, he asserted, to posit a feminine *trinitas* in the place of God the Father, creator of heaven and earth. According to Gribaldi, the Trinity is a speculative concept introduced by the Greeks, expanded in papal dreams, made worse by the Scholastics, and not found in the Scriptures. Jesus Christ is a subordinate God. "The divine seed of the Son of God or the Word took form as a human being in the Virgin Mother, *without,* however, *taking a human nature from her.*" Gribaldi, alone among the Italians, thus continued Servetus' doctrine of the heavenly flesh of Christ. All these views, Gribaldi stated, were more reasonable and Scriptural than the currently held orthodox positions.

Giorgio Biandrata (1516–1585)

Biandrata was born of a noble family in Piedmont. He was trained in medicine and was a renowned specialist in gynecology. In 1540 he was invited to the court of King Sigismund of Poland to be personal physician of the queen, the Milanese Bona Sforza. After a dozen years, he returned to practice in Italy. There he became acquainted with the views of the Reformers. In 1556, he was forced to flee the Inquisition and went to Geneva. While there, he joined the Italian congregation and soon was elected one of its elders.

At first Biandrata lived quietly and attended to his profession. Soon, however, he began to pose questions concerning the doctrine of the Trinity to the minister of the Italian congregation and to Calvin. At first Calvin patiently and seriously tried to answer Biandrata's inquiries. He wrote lengthy replies to questions concerning the meaning of such terms as person, essence, substance, and subsistence. But because Biandrata was never satisfied with his answers, Calvin concluded that Biandrata was not concerned with understanding these matters, but with stirring up dissension in the church.

Biandrata's views at this time were immature. He was more given to raising questions than to formulating answers. He basically agreed with the views of Gribaldi, though in expressing them he tried to be more subtle and cautious. He declared later in his life that he was not a theologian, but just a physician.

Others

Another nobleman from Piedmont and a fellow elder in the Italian congregation of Geneva with Biandrata was Giampaolo Alciati de la Motta (1515/20–1573). Alciati had left Piedmont at mid-century because of the rigorous policy of King Henry II of France toward heretics. He became a part of the liberal wing of the Italian congregation.

Giovanni Valenti Gentile (ca. 1520–1566) was born in Calabria. He was a renowned teacher of Latin. Attracted by the reputation of Calvin, he came to Geneva in 1556. There he joined the Italian congregation.

Calvin and the Italian Congregation

In 1557 dissension arose in the Italian congregation. Some complained that the common people were being confused by false teachings. Biandrata and some others were examined and admonished by the Consistory, but promised that they would not be punished for past errors. Biandrata sometime later, after attending a lecture by Calvin, feared that he would be arrested and fled the city. He returned only after his friend, Alciati, arranged an assurance of safe-conduct for him. The minister of the Italian congregation, Martinengo, while on his deathbed in the summer of 1557, begged Calvin and his colleagues to take action to eliminate the heresies of Gribaldi and others. Some months later, fearing that the evil was continuing to spread, several elders of the Italian congregation asked Calvin to help them. With Calvin's assistance a confession of faith was prepared designed to meet the new heretical views. A public meeting was held on May 18, 1558, at which all members of the Italian congregation were asked to sign the new confession. Calvin addressed the meeting. He then invited each person to speak freely, assuring them that there would be no prosecution for anything anyone said. A heated discussion raged for three hours. Biandrata's participation cast him in a very bad light. Alciati made an even worse impression. At one point Alciati declared that the orthodox Trinitarians "worshipped three devils worse than all the idols of popery."

Biandrata and Alciati refused to sign the confession and urged others to resist. Finally, six others joined Biandrata and Alciati in their protest and refused to sign. All other members of the congregation conformed. Gribaldi had earlier been permitted to leave the city. Soon Biandrata and Alciati fled. It was ordered that those who fled should be imprisoned if they returned to Geneva. Biandrata and Alciati eventually joined each other in Zurich, but unwelcome there they, along with Laelius Socinus, went to Poland. Calvin later wrote to a friend who had returned to Poland after a long stay in Switzerland: "Warn the good brethren, before they learn by experience what a monster Giorgio Biandrata is, or rather, how many monsters he fosters, to beware of him."

Giovanni Gentile had been noticeably absent from the May 18 meeting with Calvin, pleading ill health. On learning of the confession, he joined the objectors in refusing to sign. When Biandrata and Alciati left, however, the remaining opposition to Calvin caved in. Gentile did not know what to do. He decided to ask for a conference with Calvin. He left it professing to be convinced, but privately concluding that he would have to submit to the inevitable. After several days, all the remaining resisters, including Gentile, subscribed the confession.

Peace should have reigned in the Italian congregation. The most outspoken leaders of opposition were gone, and all the rest had conformed. But there was no peace, because the minister of the congregation continued to attack some of those who had subscribed as Arians and followers of Servetus. Furthermore, Calvin had spies in the congregation. One of them engaged Gentile in a supposedly private conversation on theology. He drew from Gentile several statements that could be interpreted as heretical. These views were reported to Calvin, who then denounced Gentile as a heretic.

Gentile was arrested and cast into prison along with another Italian who had resisted subscribing Calvin's confession. At an initial examination, the Council charged him with perjury, mutiny, sedition, and violating the promises he had given them. Gentile protested that subsequent to signing the confession he had observed the faith and agreed with the view of Calvin. Furthermore, he contended that he had always had faith in the Trinity as well as the Unity.

Another examination was held. Gentile was faced by his accusers but flatly denied their testimony. Calvin also appeared and entered the disputation. At this point Gentile requested the help of a theologian. He desired the orthodox Peter Martyr Vermigli. The Council denied his request, but granted a delay so that Gentile could prepare a confession of faith.

Subsequently Gentile produced a confession that professed belief in one God, and in Jesus Christ as his only Son. He criticized Calvin's view of the Trinity and claimed that it was really a Quaternity. He produced a list of quotations from the church fathers in support of his views. The Council and Calvin were enraged by Gentile's response. (In a letter, Calvin described Gentile as having a "portion of pride, hypocrisy, malice, and obstinate impudence greater than any other.") The Council interrogated Gentile for days, with Calvin heaping abuse on him and threatening him with capital punishment. Gentile asked for counsel to represent him, but was refused. Indeed, he was threatened with torture if he attempted to evade making direct replies.

Gentile now realized that further resistance was futile. The civil and ecclesiastical authorities, especially Calvin, were hostile to the point of violence toward him. Accordingly, Gentile asked for another opportunity to write out his views. After a period of two weeks he appeared before the Council, recanted his views, and asked the pardon of all, especially Calvin. For days in succession, Gentile was brought back to confess his errors, beg for pardon and mercy, and be assailed by yet more witnesses.

The case was referred to a committee of five lawyers. Their verdict was that Gentile was worthy of death for perjury and heresy. They doubted the sincerity of his recantation and declared that he should not be pardoned. In view of his recantation, however, they were willing to mitigate his punishment. Rather than being put to death by fire as the law required, Gentile was to be beheaded. Execution was set for the following day.

On the next day a letter came to the Council from an influential Italian residing at Lyons who interceded for Gentile. The friend blamed Biandrata, declared that Gentile was often mentally disturbed, and contended that mercy would better serve the cause of the Reformation among Italians. The Council sent the letter to Calvin. During the next two weeks more Italians protested, asking mercy for Gentile. There seemed to be a general feeling of indignation at the sentence. Finally, yielding to pressure, the Council again examined Gentile as to the sincerity of his repentance, which he espoused even more definitely than before. Accordingly, the Council reopened the case and commuted the death sentence to the performance of a public humiliation.

Now Gentile had to decide. Was he willing to appear in public half naked, throw his writings into the fire, and be led barefoot through the streets to the sound of a trumpet? He would thus concede the right of civil judges to pronounce on religion. He would be admitting that only the professionals could formulate theology. And he would acknowledge the rightness of their unreasonable and unscriptural doctrine of the Trinity. But the alternative was death. What could he do?

An Epilogue

Gentile performed his public penance—almost joyfully. He felt fortunate to escape death. Two weeks later he was given permission to go beyond the city limits. He immediately fled to Farges and joined his friends Gribaldi and Alciati. From 1558 to 1562 Gentile's reputation followed him wherever he went. He again found himself imprisoned for his beliefs at Gex and Lyons. In 1562, upon an invitation from Biandrata, Gentile joined Alciati and went to Poland.

Thus the location of the Italian anti-Trinitarian movement shifted from Switzerland to Poland. The leadership changed significantly as well. Laelius Socinus and his nephew, Faustus Socinus, who had played a minor part in the movement in Switzerland, assumed major roles in the new context. In Poland the previously vague and formless movement of opposition to Calvin became self-conscious and organized into an anti-Trinitarian denomination.

Gentile was expelled from Poland after two years and returned to Switzerland. He was summarily apprehended at Bern, convicted of heresy, deceit, and evasion. He was beheaded on September 10, 1566. This time he remained true to his convictions. As he went to the block he asserted that he willingly died as a martyr for the honor of the most high God. Times had changed in Switzerland. Apparently people were weary of the upheaval caused by religious nonconformists. Unlike the execution of Servetus, the execution of Gentile brought hardly the faintest sign of protest.

The questions remained and intensified as the years passed. What would be the long-range result of Calvin's violent opposition to anti-Trinitarianism? How effective would the use of civil power prove to be in stamping out heresy? Would all the sanctions leveled against it cause modifications in the doctrine of the anti-Trinitarians?

Bibliography

The following materials were used in the preparation of this case and are recommended for further study.

Franks, Robert S. *The Work of Christ: A Historical Study of Christian Doctrine.* London: Thomas Nelson & Sons, 1962.
Harnack, Adolf von. *History of Dogma,* Vol. VII. Translated by Neil Buchanan. Dover Publications, Inc., 1961.
Hillerbrand, Hans J. *Christendom Divided: The Protestant Reforma-

tion. Theological Resources Series. The Westminster Press, 1971.

Kot, Stanislaw. *Socinianism in Poland: The Social and Political Ideas of the Polish Anti-Trinitarians in the Sixteenth and Seventeenth Centuries.* Translated by Earl Morse Wilbur. Starr King Press, 1957.

Rees, Thomas. *The Racovian Catechism.* Lexington: The American Theological Library Association, 1962.

Schaff, Philip. *History of the Christian Church,* Vol. VIII. Wm. B. Eerdmans Publishing Company, 1958.

"Socinianism." *New Catholic Encyclopedia.* Vol. XIII, pp. 397–398.

"Socinus, Faustus, Socinians." *The New Schaff-Herzog Encyclopedia of Religious Knowledge.* Vol. X, pp. 488–493.

Wilbur, Earl Morse. *A History of Unitarianism: Socinianism and Its Antecedents.* Vol. I. Beacon Press, Inc., 1945.

Williams, George Hunston. *The Radical Reformation.* The Westminster Press, 1962.

9

The Synod of Dort
and the Arminian Controversy
(A.D. 1619)

The situation at Dort (Dordrecht), Holland, on May 6, 1619, was very tense. The main leaders of Calvinist orthodoxy from Holland and various other countries had been meeting to decide the fate of the Remonstrants. These Remonstrants were the followers of Jacob Arminius, who had called into serious question many of the chief doctrines of Reformed orthodoxy. The result had been division and strife, which threatened to tear the Dutch church in half and all of Reformed Protestantism with it. A national ecclesiastical synod had been called by the States-General to judge the doctrinal defection and decide the fate of the Remonstrants. The synod's decision was now ready. Would a synodical decision restore unity to the church? What role should the state play in deciding religious questions? What was the Biblical doctrine of salvation and how could it best be expressed? When should creeds be invoked and when could there be tolerance of diverse religious opinions? The Remonstrants had posed these questions. Now they wondered about the synod's response.

The Netherlands in the Seventeenth Century

At the opening of the seventeenth century, the United Provinces of the Netherlands were controlled by a close oligarchy of powerful burghers. There were numerous self-elected town councils, each of which exercised, within its own sphere, many of the rights of sovereignty. These councils sent delegates to the States-General of Holland. Here decisions were made which affected the entire Republic.

This case study was prepared by Professor Jack Rogers of Fuller Theological Seminary and students under his supervision: Stuart Andrews, Gary Gilman, Ted Pampeyan, Charles Schell, Ralph Wilson, Tom Wymore. It is intended as a basis for class discussion rather than to illustrate either effective or ineffective handling of a situation.

For forty years, the Dutch forces had been engaged in an exhausting, bloody conflict with Catholic Spain. The Dutch army and navy were under the leadership of Prince Maurice, who had succeeded his father, William of Orange, as general in 1584.

The outstanding leader on the home front was John of Olden Barneveldt, since 1586 the chief counselor of state. In April of 1609, Barneveldt had succeeded in negotiating a twelve-year armistice with the Spanish. The armistice was contrary to the wishes of Maurice and the high Calvinists who charged that he was a Jesuit in disguise and had been bought by Spanish gold. This truce, however, freed Maurice to take a greater interest in domestic affairs and wrought a greater polarization between the followers of Maurice and those of Barneveldt.

Jacob Arminius

The man who brought the issues of the Synod of Dort to focus was Jacob Arminius (1560–1609). His first studies were under Theodore Aemillius, a retired Roman Catholic priest who leaned toward Reformed Protestantism. Arminius spent his early teens living in Aemillius' home in Utrecht. From there at the age of sixteen Arminius went to the University of Leiden to continue his studies. It was at Leiden that he began a lifelong friendship with a fellow student, Johannes Uitenbogaert.

The time spent at Leiden was formative for the inquiring mind of the young Arminius. He was strongly influenced by Petrus Ramus (1515–1572), who was a critic of Aristotle. Ramus divorced himself from Aristotelian logic and its rigidity, and called logic a "practical" science, with emphasis on cause. Ramus introduced Arminius to the doctrine of predestination—which would later become for him a major concern. Arminius often expounded the teachings of Ramus with deep affection. Ramus' influence on him is reflected in Arminius' evaluation of his mentor: "Ramus is non-dogmatic, open to human values, and concerned with practice."

In 1581, Arminius went to Geneva to study under Theodore Beza, successor to Calvin. Beza had further "refined" Calvin's doctrine of predestination, teaching that it was *the* ground of salvation. Specifically Beza taught that predestination is an end in itself, and was essential to Reformed orthodoxy.

Arminius' many conflicts with the strict Calvinists of his day began shortly after the outset of his pulpit ministry in Amsterdam in 1588. In 1591 Arminius was requested by his church to refute the views of a Dutch layman, Coornhert, who had called into question the supralapsarian views of the orthodox Calvinists. Arminius set about to refute this "dangerous" man but upon a closer examination of the Scriptures found himself unable to defend the orthodox view. Thus, the reply never materialized—but the effect of Arminius' study in this area was to have permanent significance for the Christian church.

Arminius' change of views soon began to surface in his preaching. Challenging the traditional view of Romans, ch. 7, Arminius asserted that Paul was speaking of an unregenerate man in this passage. This brought upon him the immediate wrath of Peter Plancius, one of Holland's leading ministers and an ardent high Calvinist. Plancius questioned Arminius on the basis of the Belgic Confession and the Heidelberg Catechism, the two Reformed creeds of the Lowlands. Arminius met this challenge by denying the necessity of total allegiance to any creed. In so doing, he raised anew the problem of *sola scriptura:* Was the Scripture to be interpreted freely by men or only in the light of "legislated" creeds? Arminius held that confessions and catechisms were "revisable and reformable." He felt that the necessity of adhering to a particular confession posed an obstacle to the unity of Christians. The controversy ultimately grew so intense that Prince Maurice felt compelled to intervene. He sent Uitenbogaert, his court chaplain and Arminius' old friend, to arbitrate, but Plancius refused his proposal for compromise. Consequently, the controversy was ended by the action of the States-General, an action that surely must have been unpalatable to the high Calvinists, who were never ready to accept state interference in any ecclesiastical matter.

The Conflict with Gomarus

In 1602, Junius, professor at Leiden, died of the plague. Officiating at the funeral was Francis Gomarus, longtime professor of exegesis and dogmatics and a fervent Calvinist who taught supralapsarian predestination. This doctrine taught that before God created the world he decreed who should be saved and who should be damned. God then permitted the fall of Adam as a means of carrying out this decree. Opposed to this doctrine was infralapsarianism, which held that the decision to save and to damn was not made until after the fall of Adam and was a response to it. Realizing that Arminius was being considered to replace Junius at the university, Gomarus used the opportunity of the funeral oration to make known his opposition to the appointment. His protests, however, were of no avail, for Arminius was clearly the most qualified Dutchman for the position. So, after a long discussion with Arminius, Gomarus begrudgingly accepted him as a colleague. Arminius made clear his conception of theology in his inaugural address:

> For the theology which belongs to this world is practical and through faith: Theoretical Theology belongs to the other world, and consists of pure and unclouded vision, according to the expression of the apostle, "We walk by faith, and not by sight" (2 Cor. V,7). . . . For this reason, we must clothe the object of our theology in such a manner as may enable it to incline us to worship God, and fully to persuade and win us over to that practice.

The truce between Arminius and Gomarus was destined to be short-lived. The first dispute came in Arminius' first year. In the course of his lectures, Arminius defined predestination as the "decree of the good pleasure of God in Christ, by which he resolved within himself from all eternity, to justify, adopt and endow with everlasting life, . . . believers on whom he had decreed to bestow faith." It is evident that in this definition believers are the elect; in other words, faith precedes election.

Such teaching was, of course, not accepted by the supralapsarian Gomarus. Gomarus quickly began to put forth opposing viewpoints. The result was two opposing camps of students at the university and ministers and their congregations taking sides in the conflict throughout the country. In 1608, Gomarus added fuel to the fire by lecturing on predestination. He made it clear that he strongly opposed Arminius' views. Gomarus held that God saves some and damns others, "without any regard whatever to righteousness or sin, to obedience and disobedience, but purely of his own good pleasure to demonstrate the glory of his justice and mercy."

Increasing attacks led Arminius to request a national synod to clear himself and his sympathizer Uitenbogaert. In an oration in 1606 on reconciling religious dissensions, Arminius had expressed the opinion that a national synod should be a free convention of Christians where everybody might speak his conscience with the Scriptures as the only basis for truth. He had declared:

> May the God of truth and peace inspire the hearts of the magistrates, the people and the ministers of religion, with an ardent desire for truth and peace. May he exhibit before their eyes, in all its naked deformity, the execrable and polluting nature of dissension concerning religion; and may he affect their hearts with a serious sense of those evils which flow so copiously from it; that they may unite all their prayers, counsels, endeavors, and desires, and may direct them to one point, the removal of the

causes of such a great evil, the adoption of a mild and sanatory process, and the application of gentle remedies for healing this dissension, which are the only description of medicines of which the very weak and sickly condition of the body of the Church, and the nature of the malady, may admit. "The God of Peace" who dignifies "the peace makers" alone with the ample title of "children" (Matt. V, 9) has called us to the practice of peace.

Arminius' central idea was that of a free church founded only upon the Holy Scriptures. During the days of his professorship at Leiden, he was to expound his opinions concerning a church where the synod would "not assume to itself the authority of obtruding upon others, by force, those resolutions which may have been passed by unanimous consent." It was obvious to him that every member would agree, upon reflection, that it was possible for a synod to be both honest and in error. He quoted Tertullian: "Nothing is less a religious business than to employ coercion about religion."

Arminius' request for a synod was denied, but he was allowed to confront Gomarus at The Hague in 1608. Both men were officially exhorted by Barneveldt to place the unity of church and nation above all other priorities. Among those present was the eminent Dutch jurist Hugo Grotius, who left the meeting very sympathetic to Arminius. Gomarus, however, was convinced that Arminius was extremely heretical and thereby refused to be quieted.

Later that same year Arminius was allowed to present his grievances to a meeting of the States-General. There he attacked the orthodox Reformed Church doctrine of predestination as "contrary and repugnant to the nature of God" which "made God the author of sin, hindered sorrow for sin, lessened the earnest desire for piety and good works." He denied that this doctrine was found in the Scriptures or the church fathers and charged that this extreme predestination doctrine was in fact the cause of the division within the church.

Replies from his opponents were immediate, and Arminius' supporters rose quickly to his defense. His health now failing, he had time for one last clash with Gomarus before his death. Arminius continued his debate with Gomarus in The Hague. The issues were the same, with Gomarus questioning Arminius' view of the free will of man. The conference, however, was halted abruptly by Arminius' sudden failure in health. On October 19, 1609, Arminius died, bringing his own part in the dispute to an end.

Many in the United Provinces were hopeful that Arminius' death would end the strife that disturbed the nation. Such, however, was not the case. Arguments over Arminius' successor at Leiden caused considerable uproar, including a condemnation of the Arminians by James I of England, an important military ally of the United Provinces. Finally, Gomarus left for a position at Middleburg in protest against the appointment of Simon Episcopius, a leading Arminian, to fill the chair vacated by Arminius. Gomarus was replaced by the Calvinist Polyander.

In January, 1610, the court chaplain Uitenbogaert brought together the Arminian leaders and drew up a Remonstrance against the high Calvinists which consisted of five articles stating their variance with the Reformed Church teaching. These five articles were directed against four specific doctrines of the extreme Calvinists: the supralapsarian decree, the notion that grace was irresistible, the idea that Christ died only for the elect, and the concept that the saints could not fall from grace.

The Remonstrant Position

The Arminians felt that the Calvinist doctrine of decrees, whether supralapsarian or infralapsarian, was contrary to the nature of God. The problem with the supralapsarian view was that it made God the author of sin. Arminius' own statement concerning this view is typical:

> He therefore determined to create them upright, to lay down a law for them, and ordained that they should sin and become wicked, in order that He might in this way attend the end of creation, that is, to carry out their reprobation in damning them for His glory. In this process, I say, they ascribe far baser things to God than if they should simply say He created creatures in order to damn them.

The infralapsarian view came under the Arminian attack because it still made the reprobation of some men a "positive" decree. That is, God deliberately and arbitrarily decreed that some men would be reprobate and thus destined for hell without giving them an opportunity to make a decision. To answer this "attack" upon God's perfect and loving nature the Arminians proposed "conditional predestination." This view states that God's predestining men to salvation or damnation was based upon his foreknowledge of their conduct. The Calvinists reacted to such a view with horror, considering it a dark reproach upon God's sovereignty.

The Arminians' view of predestination led them naturally to the question of God's grace. In order to maintain their doctrine of a God who did not violate man's freedom by predestining him arbitrarily to a fate with no say in the matter themselves, the Arminians had to reject the Calvinist doctrine of irresistible grace. They therefore proposed that the grace of God was absolutely necessary for a man to come to salvation, but could be rejected and resisted. They found support for this view in the Scriptures which spoke of resisting the Holy Spirit. The Calvinists again viewed this as an affront to the absolute sovereignty of God.

The question of whether or not Christ died only for the elect also grew out of the question of predestination. Arminius found support for his contention that God had not deliberately predestined men to hell in the teaching of Christ's dying for all men. Arminius' followers developed this theme into one deliberately aimed at refuting the Calvinist proposal that Christ died only for the predestined elect.

The Arminians also questioned on the basis of the Scriptures the Calvinist doctrine of the perseverance of believers. Arminius felt that certain Scriptures brought into question the contention that a believer could not turn against the God who had called him and be ultimately lost. His followers questioned the doctrine even more and proposed that "falling away" was indeed a possibility for the believer. The Calvinists felt that this was an attack upon the assurance of the believer and a rejection of the doctrine of election. What assurance could there be if one could fall away? How can God elect men if some may ultimately reject him? The Arminians replied that the believer had a full assurance of all the grace necessary to persevere and that God had elected only those he knew would persevere.

These issues dealt with the age-old problem of the relationship of God's sovereignty to man's free will. The Calvinists were anxious to protect God's sovereignty from any erosion. The Arminians, on the other hand, were chiefly concerned with the freedom of man to make a choice. They found this doctrine best supported by those passages of the Scriptures which stressed God's justice and love. There was, however, another issue involved. This was the issue of the Scripture's place in the church. The early Reformers had proclaimed a doctrine of *sola scriptura.* The Arminians were reacting at least partly to the orthodox party's imposition of extra-Biblical creeds upon the church. Arminius had said to Uitenbogaert, concerning one Calvinist's assertion that the Scriptures had to be interpreted in the light of the Heidelberg Catechism and the Belgic Confession, "How could one state more clearly that they were determined to canonize these two human writings, and to set them up as the two idolatrous calves at Dan and Beersheba?"

The articles were therefore calling into question more than the orthodox view of the sovereignty of God. They were also raising the question of the right of men to interpret Scripture freely.

Events Leading to the Synod of Dort

In July of 1610 at the urging of Barneveldt, the States-General accepted the articles of the Remonstrants as being consistent with the Reformed faith. The ensuing uproar brought charges and countercharges. In 1611 the Remonstrant-dominated states moved to silence opposition in the churches to the disputed five points, though they were soon forced to back down. When attempts at unification failed, the Counter-Remonstrants began to leave the church. The Remonstrants prevented the seceding Calvinist congregations from taking the buildings, however, for they soon expected to control all the churches.

The doctrinal disputes revealed equally deep-seated differences about church polity. There was growing Calvinist resistance to pressure from the state to control the appointments of pastors and professors. The Remonstrants, who were well represented among the national political leaders, were strong advocates of state influence over the church. Uitenbogaert expressed their fear that a strong ecclesiastical hierarchy of Calvinists would banish the idea of toleration which had played a significant role in Dutch national life.

Prince Maurice had been generally neutral in the religious disputes up to this time. When, however, in 1616 Barneveldt asked him to sustain the States-General's ruling to punish dissenters as disturbers of the peace, Maurice declared that he had taken an oath as general to defend the Reformed faith, and took a firm position at the head of the Counter-Remonstrant party, even though it was suspected that his own religious inclinations were Arminian. Since the majority of the people were Calvinists, it was necessary that he stand with them if he was to gain control of the state from his "enemy" Barneveldt.

The clash between Barneveldt and Maurice rapidly edged the country toward civil war. Barneveldt succeeded in getting the States-General to approve the raising of local militia who swore allegiance to it, without mention of Maurice. But pressure for a national synod to discuss the Remonstrants' position grew, and Maurice finally pressured the States-General to call a synod to meet in Dort in November, 1618.

In January, 1618, Prince Maurice began a systematic tour of Dutch towns, dismissing unfriendly magistrates and appointing high Calvinists in their place. By July, the representation of the Counter-Remonstrants had increased to the point that the States-General ordered the militia disbanded. Maurice now had the only armed force in the Netherlands. In August, Barneveldt, Grotius, and other Remonstrant leaders were arrested and Uitenbogaert fled the country.

The appointment of Calvinist magistrates by Maurice ensured that by the time of the synod in November, of the delegates from the United Provinces only the three from Utrecht were Remonstrants. All the twenty-four foreign divines were distinguished for their ardent defense of absolute predestination. Representatives from Lutheran churches were not invited.

The Synod of Dort

John Bogerman, archenemy of the Remonstrants, was chosen as president of the Synod when it convened on November 13, 1618. As the chief figure, Bogerman added real color to the Synod. He was described as being "a very remarkable man physically and mentally." He was a powerful speaker, "and his gestures, when he was excited (which was not seldom, for he was a man of strong passions), were very impressive." The Synod moved immediately to cite fourteen representatives of the Remonstrants to appear before it. The delegates from Utrecht were removed from their seats. From the first moments of the Synod it was apparent that both the civil authority of the States-General and the ecclesiastical authority of the Reformed Church were going to treat the Remonstrants not as brothers whose views were to be discussed, but as heretics to be judged.

Simon Episcopius led the party of Remonstrants who were ushered into the Synod fourteen days later to sit at the long table in the center of the hall. Episcopius had done much to advance the Remonstrant cause since Arminius' death. Possessing a superb gift for organization of doctrine, he utilized his position as professor at Leiden to its fullest capacity to propagate Remonstrant teachings. He had been especially powerful in his arguments for religious toleration and for the supremacy of the state. He had echoed Arminius in his denial of the authority of creeds as well as adhering to much of Arminius' theology. Episcopius' address to the Synod was moving and eloquent, yet the impact of the message was lost. Bogerman confused the issue by squabbling with the Remonstrants about the differences in the spoken version of the address from the text which he had previously been given.

The Remonstrants protested strongly against the legitimacy of the

Synod. They questioned how a synod made up solely of their avowed enemies could impartially judge their views. On December 10 the Remonstrants read a statement prepared by Episcopius which declared that the Remonstrants did not recognize the members of the Synod as lawful judges, since the great majority were their professed enemies. Episcopius further stated that the members of the Synod and their constituents were responsible for the unfortunate schism in the churches of the land. Their objections overruled, the Remonstrants were ordered to give elaborate oral expression of their views. They refused to accede to this demand unless they could be heard on the actual points in dispute. The Synod would not allow this, because it would imply an equal conference, not a judgment on the Remonstrants, and would also expose the divisions among the Calvinists between the supralapsarians and the infralapsarians. The Synod was afraid to exhibit these divisions, because it wanted the decrees of the Synod to be accepted in all the Reformed churches throughout Europe and England.

Finally, on January 14, it became obvious that the impasse could not be broken. The Remonstrants declared that their consciences would not permit them to yield their position on the five articles. President Bogerman grew livid with anger, his whole frame trembling with violent emotion. He roared to the Remonstrants in Latin expletives: "You are dismissed! Get out! You began with a lie, you have ended with a lie! Go!" Episcopius and the other Remonstrants retired with the words: "God will judge between me and the Synod. . . . I appeal to the throne of Christ." One of the Remonstrants, as he neared the door, shouted, "Go out from the assemblies of the wicked."

After the expulsion of the Remonstrants from the Synod, an examination of their doctrines was begun, culminating on April 24, 1619, with a solemn sentence of condemnation against their tenets. The Synod then gave itself to formulating its own response to the Remonstrants. Although President Bogerman prepared a statement of the faith of the Reformed Church, the Synod, uneasy about his extreme views, desired a committee document representing a more moderate position. The Canons of Dort were given under five heads, each corresponding to the opposing Remonstrant articles. They set forth clearly the doctrine of predestination, but not in the supralapsarian sense. On May 6, 1619, an overflow crowd jammed into the Great Church of Dort. The Canons of Dort and the *Censura ecclesiastica* against the Remonstrants were read. The Remonstrants, no longer present, were eager to know the form of the judgment against them. Would these documents restore unity to the majority of Reformed churches? What might the state do to enforce conformity? Had an acceptable consensus been achieved in expressing the Biblical teaching on salvation? Might this creed be imposed to the exclusion of all other religious opinions? These questions filled the minds of the ejected Remonstrants as they awaited the decision.

AN EPILOGUE

The sentence of the Synod of Dort against the Remonstrants on May 6, 1619, was confirmed two months later by the States-General. Two hundred Remonstrant ministers were deposed. Eighty of those who rebelled were exiled. Those who held Remonstrant doctrines were forbidden to meet.

After the public reading of the Canons in the Great Church of Dort, the presence of the foreign Reformed theologians from England, various German states, and Switzerland was no longer deemed necessary. On May 9 the foreign dignitaries were given a grand send-off banquet. Some of them accepted an invitation of the States-General to visit Utrecht to observe the conclusion of another aspect of the Remonstrant controversy. Barneveldt, Hogerbeets, and Grotius, the Remonstrant leaders arrested in August of 1618, had endured a long-drawn-out trial. In April of 1619 a verdict of guilty was passed against them by judges who were chosen from among their avowed enemies. Imposition of their sentences had been stayed, however, until the Synod was concluded. On May 14, 1619, the head of Barneveldt rolled on the scaffold beneath the ax of the state executioner. One of the spectators, a Swiss pastor, remarked: "The Canons of Dordrecht have shot it off."

Hugo Grotius was sentenced to life imprisonment in the castle at Louvestein. Grotius was indeed politically and personally aligned with the Arminians. Theologically, however, he had been developing his own distinctive stance. In addition to the Calvinist-Arminian debate raging in Holland, there was considerable anabaptist, anti-Trinitarian sentiment. Faustus Socinus' work was known. The Polish anti-Trinitarian Racovian Catechism had been published in 1605. No less a person than James I of England had accused the Arminian professor Simon Episcopius of Socinianism. In response to this challenge Grotius published in 1617 *A Defense of the Catholic Faith Concerning the Satisfaction of Christ, Against Faustus Socinus.* Now as he faced imprisonment for his beliefs Grotius pondered his position. Could his view of the atonement really offer a middle way between high Calvinism and Socinianism? Would another way of framing doctrine be more effective than the "practical" approach of the Remonstrants or the "speculative" style of the Dort Calvinists? Could those like himself who were identified with the condemned Remonstrants exert any significant theological influence in the future?

Hugo Grotius (1583–1645)

Hugo Grotius was born in Delft of an influential family in 1583. At the age of twelve he went to the University of Leiden, where he became deeply influenced by humanism under Joseph Juste Scaliger, the French classicist and humanist. At the age of fifteen Grotius accompanied John of Olden Barneveldt to Paris and soon after became established as a lawyer. At the age of eighteen he was appointed historian of the States-General. In 1607, at the age of twenty-four, he was named fiscal advocate for the Province of Holland. In 1613 he was appointed pensionary of Rotterdam and represented that city in the States of Holland and in the States-General of the United Provinces. During this period he began to take a keen interest in theological questions. He sided with the Arminians and supported Olden Barneveldt's policy of moderation. Because of these positions he incurred the hostility of Prince Maurice, now the self-appointed leader of the Calvinists. Grotius responded in 1614 with publication of a *Resolution for Peace in the Church*.

The Governmental Theory of the Atonement

Grotius' training as a historian and jurist led him to seek a different way of formulating the meaning of Christ's saving work for us. Identified as he was with the Arminians, Grotius' deepest concern was to find a middle way between the dilemma of Calvinism and its Socinian antithesis.

The Calvinist view was rooted in the medieval "satisfaction" theory of Anselm. As modified by the Calvinist Reformers, this doctrine taught that Christ's death was penal and vicarious. Because man's sin made him guilty of transgressing the law of God, justice required that a penalty be paid. Christ's death was considered to be a vicarious sufficient payment for all sin. This payment was efficacious only for the sins of the elect for whom it was made and to whom alone it was applied.

Socinianism denied, along with Duns Scotus and Abelard, that God's nature demanded punishment for sin. Nor did it hold that a penalty due to one person could justly or effectively be paid by another. The work of Christ became an example to man, teaching him the way of self-sacrificing love.

In developing his view of salvation Grotius reached back to three classical sources: Aristotle's philosophy of the state, Roman law, and the political philosophy of Thomas Aquinas. The basic work of Christ was to uphold divine law and defend the just government of the universe. Just as an earthly magistrate, God could pardon anyone if he chose to do so. The law that sinners have transgressed is not "natural law," inherent in the nature of God. Rather, our sins have broken "positive law," which is a product of God's will to which he is not bound and which he can suspend or alter as he pleases. Hence, God freely forgives sinners, dispensing with the penalty of death which sinners deserve. Why, then, did Christ die? Because, according to Grotius, God as the ruler of the universe had to see that order was kept in his realm. The breaking of even positive law could not be taken lightly. Therefore Christ's death is a nominal, though not an exact, equivalent penalty paid for the breaking of divine law. Grotius contended: "This act of the Father, so far as it relates to the law, is relaxation, but so far as it relates to the criminal is remission." Thus in Christ's death God evidences his hatred of sin, his mercy toward sinners, and his insistence that the laws of the universe be maintained.

The Aftermath of the Synod of Dort

Grotius occupied himself during his imprisonment with philological and theological studies. In March of 1621, at his request, a large chest of his books was delivered to him. By prior arrangement with his wife and a servant, Grotius concealed himself in the empty book chest and was carried from the castle, making good his escape. He fled to Paris and lived there for many years under the protection of Louis XIII. From 1635 until his death in 1645 he acted as the Swedish ambassador to Paris. In 1622 Grotius wrote an apologetic work, *De veritate religionis Christianae*. In it he followed the line of rational and evidential argument developed in an early work of Socinus. Grotius intended his work as a practical manual to help sailors refute pagans and Mohammedans by establishing the superiority of Christianity over other religions. In 1625 Grotius authored *De jure belli et pacis* which earned him the title of "Father of International Law." In 1642, shortly before his death, Grotius published *Annotationes in Vetus et Novum Testamentum*. It opened a new approach to Biblical exegesis by using literary criticism based on comparing Biblical statements with passages from Greek and Latin authors. Grotius continued, nevertheless, to stress the need for ecclesiastical tradition as a guide to a correct understanding of the Scriptures.

The Canons of Dort were officially received by Holland, France, the Palatinate, and Switzerland, though they were merely countenanced by England and Brandenburg. James I of England swayed heavily to Arminianism in his later years and in 1622 forbade the preaching of the doctrine of predestination in England. After the death of Maurice in 1625, the exiled Remonstrants were allowed to return. A decree of 1630 authorized them to build churches and schools. Thus well before Grotius' death he had an opportunity to reflect on the questions that were so pressing at the time of his imprisonment: Had he developed a viable alternative view of the atonement between Calvinism and Socinianism? Was his formulation of doctrine on the model of Roman law a success? Could the Remonstrants now once more expect to have significant influence in Holland and elsewhere?

BIBLIOGRAPHY

The following materials were used in the preparation of this case and are recommended for further study.

Bangs, Carl. *Arminius.* Abingdon Press, 1971.

Bettenson, Henry, ed. *Documents of the Christian Church.* Oxford University Press, 1947.

Calder, Frederick. *Memoirs of Simon Episcopius.* Methodist Episcopal Church, 1837.

Hansen, Maurice G. *The Reformed Church in the Netherlands.* Board of Publications of the Reformed Church in America, 1884.

Harrison, A. W. *Arminianism.* London: Gerald Duckworth & Co., Ltd., 1937.

McClintock, John. "Dort, Synod of," in *Cyclopedia of Biblical, Theological, and Ecclesiastical Literature.* Harper & Brothers, 1868.

McCulloh, G. O. *Man's Faith and Freedom: The Theological Influence of Jacobus Arminius.* Abingdon Press, 1962.

Neve, J. L. *History of Protestant Theology,* Vol. II. Muhlenberg Press, Publishers, 1946.

Nichols, James. *The Writings of Jacob Arminius.* Grand Rapids: Baker Book House, 1956.

Shedd, William G. F. *History of Christian Doctrine.* Edinburgh: T. & T. Clark, 1869.

Walker, Williston. *A History of the Christian Church.* Charles Scribner's Sons, 1970.

10
The Shakers (A.D. 1774)

Elder John Rankin wondered at the options and the right way to proceed. This decision, like all community decisions, should reflect not just the ethical position of the Shakers but their faith about the coming Kingdom as well. The problem was not just a matter of money, either, it represented a dealing with human lives and destinies. As a Shaker in the South Union colony, in southern Kentucky, he confronted perhaps the most complicated situation yet. Thus he sought direction from the Central Ministry of the Society of Believers, the Shakers' leadership. What should he do?

1. Shall money or property which has been obtained by the sale of Negro slaves be refused or accepted by the church of Christ?
2. If refused, how far removed from the sweat and blood of the slave must money and property be in order to render such money or property acceptable to the church? Our sugar and coffee come directly from the toiling slave through his master, and is acceptable. Should money be equally so?
3. There is a sister of twenty-five years' standing in the society and fifteen years in the church, whose father, in Tennessee, being the owner of some slaves, died intestate. By the laws of that state, "Made and provided" the court has to sell the property, slaves included. The proceeds of this sale brings to the heirs, $2000.00 each. We have received for the heir who is with us, $1600.00 and soon will have the balance. When question No. 1 is answered we will know what to do.

This case study was prepared by Professor Louis Weeks of the Louisville Presbyterian Theological Seminary, as a basis for class discussion rather than to illustrate either effective or ineffective handling of a situation.

Antebellum America, with its rampant slavery system, made the simple life very complex. Rankin, who evidently had left the Presbyterians to join the Shakers because he was convinced of their doctrine concerning God and the salvation of people, now still had to deal with the "world" in a fair and Christian manner. Shaker doctrines about Christ and salvation would affect the decision rendered by the Central Ministry also. Since they represented the continuing authority of Mother Ann Lee herself, he turned to them for help.

Shakers had come to the New World in 1774, a tattered band with Ann Lee at their head. Mother Ann, as she was already called, had experienced much tragedy as a child working in English factories, and as a young woman married to Abraham Standerin, a blacksmith. The four children born to them all died in infancy, a succession of events that was compounded by the difficult relationship she experienced with her spouse. But she found spiritual resources in the company of a group of radical Quakers and soon began leading them, both in and out of prison where they spent occasional sojourns for "disturbing the peace" and other nonconformist activities. Gradually she assumed the title "Mother of the New Creation" and formulated the plans to immigrate to America. Shakers moved to capitalize on the revival movements that made their converts open to a new theology.

The new millennium was dawning, preached Ann Lee and her little band, located in Niskeyuna, near Albany, New York. Conversions to Shakerism increased, and despite incarceration during a portion of the Revolution (patriots mistook her pacifism for Toryism), she led missions in the surrounding areas until her death in 1784. Joseph Meacham, and later Sister Lucy Wright, led the forming communitarian movement in developing Ann Lee's theology and in establishing the most successful utopian attempt during the nineteenth century.

Ann Lee's teaching was simple, as was the life she urged on those following her. Confession she understood as the "doorway" to salvation, and celibacy as the "cross" borne by community members. Acts, ch. 2, especially vs. 42–47, proved the guiding authority for the common life of believers. As their "parents" the Quakers, Shakers took seriously the need for America to end the practice of slavery. They likewise took no oaths and bore no arms. Life was to be lived on a higher plane by believers, who would neither take nor give in marriage. It was to be a "resurrection" order of things, in which women and men shared equally in bearing responsibility. Ann Lee was soon taken to be the female incarnation of the Christ principle (if indeed she did not teach her messiahship personally). After the order in Acts, membership was first in a novitiate family, then in a junior family, and finally in the church family.

As Shakerism moved southward, it encountered new problems. Missionaries, testifying at the revival services, had come to Kentucky in 1805. In Gasper, Logan County, they convicted and convinced the Rev. John Rankin of the need for his conversion to Shakerism. He joined, with a number from his Presbyterian congregation. Many of these new members joined the colony forming at South Union, Kentucky. Another Shaker colony grew in Pleasant Hill, in Mercer County. At the height of popularity in the 1850's there were more than six thousand Shakers in the United States, including membership in the two Kentucky colonies. But growth in these "western" areas was limited by disease, trouble with Indians, and social attitudes of the people. Malaria proved a real factor in the demise of Indiana outposts, an enterprise interrupted by attacks and threats of attacks from the indigenous Americans.

But the main problem for Southern colonies of Shakers proved to be the institution of slavery, and the attitudes of white neighbors to the Shaker doctrines of human equality. In Northern colonies blacks evidently were few, but were accepted as members of the communities on an equal basis with whites. The South Union, Kentucky, colony settled for a separate black family, with its own black elder. One way of dealing with the institution, according to Elder Eads, would be to put slaves on "decent Shaker wages" and let them buy their freedom as soon as possible. In the situation confronted by Rankin, difficulties arose because slaves brought to Kentucky could not be freed easily—the laws were complicated.

Shakers believed that their problems would be short-lived, however. They expected the realization of the millennium that they knew was dawning. Now that the "second coming" of Christ, whose female incarnation was in Mother Ann, had occurred, the apocalyptic passages applied. By several accounts, that is why Shakers hung their portable furniture each night on the pegs around each room—preparing the way of the Lord. Should the Christ with the angels come during the night, they would have no impediments in their traffic pattern. And, mundanely, such practice made the cleaning of the rooms a simpler process. Mixing the eschatological and the utilitarian was their desire. In the words of Shaker John Dunlavy's *Manifesto:* "It is the duty, the indispensible duty of all those who hear the gospel testimony, to open their ears with freedom and without prejudice, while its ministers reason with them. . . . People would rather salvation could be had in some other way." God had chosen a straight and narrow path of Shakerism, therefore people should consider "whether the opposition [sic] in their own breast be not that which renders the gospel of Christ's second appearing, dark and objectionable, more than any lack of evidence or conviction."

Believing as they did in the immediate coming of the "new creation" of which they were a part, Shakers found themselves after 1838 communicating with their departed leaders—Mother Ann, Elder Joseph, and Eldress Lucy. In addition, their worship centered on the coming perfection of all life. The gifts—all of them—were perceived as resurrection gifts. God gave to their well-ordered lives a temporal and eternal meaning. This they celebrated in song and dance, worship and work.

One of the songs, a favorite in Kentucky, celebrated both the joy of their postmillennialism and the hope of eternal life:

> Lo, out on yonder plain
>   In holiness and beauty
> A lovely bright angel's train
>   Engaged in heavenly duty
> The scene surpasses earth's delight
>   No mortal can express it
> Celestial Cherubs clothed in white
>   And by Jehovah blessed.
>
> Earth may cease to spread her charms
>   Her pleasures can't allure me
> I'm bound to reach the lovely arms
>   Of those who are gone before me
> Tho all creation should decay
>   And thousands be offended
> I'll hold my birthright watch and pray
>   Until my work is ended.

It was in this attitude that Elder Rankin asked for help from the Central Ministry. Should he accept the money from the "carnal" world and compromise with the institution of slavery? Should he seek primarily the good benefits of Shaker promises for the affected slaves? Should his concern rather be for the solvency of the community? And how would his doctrines about God, Jesus Christ, and salvation affect his decision?

Bibliography

The following materials were used in the preparation of this case and are recommended for future study.

Andrews, E. D. *The People Called Shakers.* Oxford University Press, 1953.

Desroche, Henri. *The American Shakers.* Translated and edited by J. Savacool. University of Massachusetts Press, 1971.

Dunlavy, John. *The Manifesto.* 1818. Reprint. AMS Press, Inc., 1972.

Gibson, M. *Shakerism in Kentucky.* Cynthiana, Ky.: Hobson Press, Inc., 1942.

Hutton, M. H. *Old Shakertown and the Shakers.* Harrodsburg, Ky.: Herald Press, 1936.

Marshall, Mary. *A Portraiture of Shakerism.* 1822. Reprint. AMS Press, Inc., 1972.

11

The Heresy of John McLeod Campbell
(A.D. 1831)

The Meeting of the General Assembly, 1831

Meeting at Edinburgh in May of 1831, the commissioners of the General Assembly of the Church of Scotland had a hard decision to make. John McLeod Campbell, the minister of the parish of Row, had been accused in the previous year before his presbytery of holding and promulgating the doctrine that assurance is of the essence of faith and also the universality of Christ's atonement and pardon, contrary to Scripture and the Westminster Confession of Faith. The Presbytery of Dumbarton had found the charges proven. The Synod of Glasgow and Ayr had upheld the verdict. As the court of final appeal the General Assembly had the task of considering the charges, reviewing the decisions of the presbytery and the synod, and passing judgment on a minister whose saintliness and love of the gospel of Christ had been attested to by the majority of the elders, members, and adherents of his congregation.

The Theological Climate of Scotland in the 1830's

When the Reformation came to Scotland in the sixteenth century, Calvinism achieved an ascendancy unequaled anywhere else in Europe. In doctrine, the influence of John Calvin's *Institutes of the Christian Religion* dominated and in the following century was the architectonic principle underlying the Westminster Confession of Faith. Commitment to the Confession became increasingly rigid, and from 1690 a generation of ordinands was required to subscribe

This case study was prepared by Professor Ross Mackenzie of Union Theological Seminary in Virginia as a basis for class discussion rather than to illustrate either effective or ineffective handling of a situation.

it as "founded upon the Word of God." Throughout the eighteenth century it was regarded as a touchstone of Calvinistic orthodoxy, especially by the heirs of the Covenanters and by the Seceders. As late as the 1830's the Shorter Catechism was taught in all schools.

In his *Institutes*, Calvin had defined predestination as "God's eternal decree, by which he compacted with himself what he wills to become of each man. . . . Eternal life is foreordained for some, eternal damnation for others." The Confession of Faith set this same doctrine forth in Chapters III and XVIII. Some felt that the Confession taught that God not only willed salvation for the elect, and effectually leads them to faith and glory, but willed the damnation of the nonelect, whose very sins were divinely ordained. In the words of a Seceder document of 1754: "Our Lord Jesus Christ hath redeemed none others, by his death, but the elect only."

In explaining Christ's death and the meaning of his atonement, orthodox Calvinists held that the Lord's sufferings had infinite penal value as a sacrifice for sin. His willingness to endure the cross and die for the sins of the world was imputed to those who were the objects of his mediatorial work. But the idea that Christ sacrificed himself for the sins of all was hard to reconcile with the idea that God has willed salvation only for the elect. The solution of the theologians was to teach that Christ had died *sufficienter pro omnibus, efficaciter pro electis* ("sufficiently for all, efficaciously for the elect"). They separated the purchase of Christ's death from its application. Only the elect have redemption applied to them.

Yet within the eighteenth century it was only a vocal minority that regarded scholastic Calvinism as the only permissible teaching. To many it seemed that such rigorous views and the requirement of subscribing the Confession inhibited constructive thought. When the influence of the Enlightenment first began to dawn in Scotland, the new thinkers began to show that the rigid theological foundations of the church's faith were also fragile. Among the Scottish deists there was a will to discard every form of intolerance, all that was mysterious and miraculous about Christianity, and every superfluous doctrine. The philosopher David Hume had entered the domain of morals and religion and shocked the pious with his skepticism. As early as 1738 he had speculated in his *A Treatise of Human Nature* that people can have no knowledge of anything beyond their own ideas and impressions. In his *The Natural History of Religion* he argued pungently against the case upon which natural theology was built, and said, of religion: "The whole is a riddle, an enigma, an inexplicable mystery."

For all his skepticism, however, Hume had no desire to wound the feelings of his country, or grieve or offend believers. But there were many by the turn of the century who agreed that his vigorous skepticism was beginning to have two opposite effects. It was clear, they said, that he had discredited Deism. But his assault on the religious faith that Scotland had known was beginning to produce a skeptical atheism.

Hume, it was also widely conceded, had helped to produce within the church a questioning about fundamentals. What—it was beginning to be asked—is the ground of belief? What is God, what is the meaning of Christ, and what can be firmly believed?

Parties Within the Scottish Church

Two parties existed in the Scottish Church at the beginning of the nineteenth century, the Moderates and the Evangelicals. Since 1752 the Moderates had fast gained ground in attaining dominance in the General Assembly. They were characterized by a mood of tolerance, an absence of dogmatism, and a care for the peace and unity of the church. Though they professed strict Westminster orthodoxy, the Moderates were clearly sympathetic to the spirit of free inquiry and criticism that characterized the Enlightenment. Their adherence to the sterner forms of Calvinism, notably its preoccupation with the punishment of sexual offenders, was nominal rather than real, for they took a somewhat milder view toward the sins of the flesh than the rigorists among the Evangelicals.

For different reasons the Evangelicals also parted company with Calvin at certain theological crossroads. They were faithful in assembling with their fellows for prayer and Bible study. Where they did not repudiate, they were uneasy about the connection between the church and the state, preferring the idea of a gathered congregation. Their love of Scripture and their emphasis on conversion led them to form missionary societies—and to receive the criticism of the more orthodox Calvinists, who regarded such a step as inconsistent with the doctrine of election. "If it were not true that Christ died for the heathen," asked one of the Evangelicals, "pray, what gospel is the missionary to preach when he lands on a foreign shore?"

If the Evangelicals could point to any theological writing which adequately set forth their favorite doctrine of free grace, it was the controversial *Marrow of Modern Divinity*. This work had first been published at London in 1646, the work of Edward Fisher of Brazenose College. It was in the form of a dialogue between Evangelista, a minister, and three of his people: Nomista, a legalist who regarded the Christian life as obedience to God's law; Antinomista, who relied on grace and sat loosely to moral obligation; and a young Christian, Neophyta. A new edition of the *Marrow* appeared in 1718, but within two years it was condemned by the General Assembly as containing five distinct heresies: that assurance was of the essence of faith; that the atonement was universal; that holiness was not necessary to salvation; that the fear of punishment and hope of reward were not motives of a believer's obedience; and that the Christian is not under the rule of the law. The declaration of the Assembly was clear: "The doctrine of universal atonement and pardon through the death of Christ, and also the doctrine that assurance is of the essence of faith and necessary to salvation, are contrary to the holy scriptures and to the Confession of Faith."

The Evangelicals persisted, nevertheless, in preaching for conversion. William McCulloch, warmed by the news of the revival in New England, preached conversion and the experience of being born again to the crowds who flocked to Cambuslang. On one occasion thirty thousand people were gathered in the fields, to the astonishment even of George Whitefield, who came in 1742 to see if what he had been told was true.

In the 1820's and 1830's the writings of Thomas Erskine of Linlathen showed him to be in sympathy with the views of the Evangelicals. An Episcopal layman who had been educated for the bar, Erskine had retired from the law to pursue a life of contemplation and study on his family estate. So far as Calvinism honored God as all in all and infinitely above the creature, Erskine honored it. What he could not accept was its conception of God as the one in whom power is paramount and therefore its restriction of the love of God. He repudiated also the Calvinistic version of the atonement which regarded Christ's death as the price paid to satisfy the demands of divine justice. Christ died for everyone, he said, as the head of the whole mass of human nature. "I am sure," he wrote to a correspondent, "that the sorrow which holy love feels for sin is the true and essential and divine medicine for sin."

John McLeod Campbell

John McLeod Campbell was born at Armaddy House on May 4, 1800, the son of the minister of Kilninver, Donald Campbell. Since his mother died when he was six, he had few memories of her; but life in his father's home was a happy one, as it was to be also in his own home after his marriage. His education was received at the Universities of Glasgow and Edinburgh, and in 1825 he was presented to the parish of Row, a quiet rural community with a number of ancient ruined chapels, by his patron, the Duke of Argyll.

Campbell entered his ministry on strictly orthodox lines. He professed loyalty to the Confession of Faith, but shortly he began to see that many in his congregation were hesitating before barriers. For one, the barrier was a lack of what seemed to be true repentance; for a second, insufficient faith; for yet another, the sense of not being good enough. None questioned the power of Christ to save, or even his willingness: their doubts concerned themselves. In his preaching and pastoral ministry, therefore, Campbell—"a beautiful and serious soul," his own son called him—urged his hesitant parishioners to ponder on God's feelings toward them rather than scrutinize their own feelings toward God.

Among the friends of the minister of Row was Edward Irving, a tall, genial eccentric with black bushy hair and a marked squint. In the years just after Campbell came to his parish Irving had been part of a circle of fifty people meeting to study the prophetic books of the Bible. Out of the conferences the Catholic Apostolic Church was born. One Sunday in March 1830, Mary Campbell of Row, no relative of the minister, began to speak in an unknown tongue and continued for an hour or so. Irving's own church in London was often at this time the scene of excited disorder.

Irving had met Campbell in Edinburgh when he came north to deliver a series of lectures on the book of The Revelation in 1828, and the two had spoken at length on the assurance of faith and the universality of Christ's atonement. But many in and out of Scotland regarded Irving's views on the humanity of Christ as dangerously unorthodox, and in 1832 his presbytery in London convicted him of heresy.

At Row the preaching of Campbell increasingly centered on two recurring themes. The first of these was that Christ had died for all, God's gift for every human being. "Believe in the forgiveness of sins," he said, "not so that they may be forgiven, *but because they are forgiven!*" As the congregation listened to the novel but consoling words, Campbell showed them an image of Christ that they had not seen before. "How did Christ express his love and show that he loved every man as himself?" With such a question the preacher began to set out his understanding of the atonement:

> Was it not by his dying as well as by all his other doings that he set forth his love? If, then, Christ loved all, and if it thus appears that God loved all—, and if Christ's actings expressed his love, which is God's love to all, then this great act of humbling himself to the death, even the death of the cross, must be expressive of

the love of Christ to all men, and therefore of the love of God to all men.

As partaker of our humanity, Christ took to himself the sin of the world, and his confession of that sin in our humanity—not our doubtful sorrow—is the ground of our forgiveness. "He has taken the nature and become the brother of those whose sins he confesses before their Father, and he feels concerning their sins what, as the holy One of God, and as perfectly loving God and man, he must feel."

With Campbell, assurance of faith was the corollary of this doctrine of the atonement. He used to say to his people, "If you knew the mind of God towards you as the gospel reveals it, if you only knew as really your own the unsearchable riches which you have in Christ —you must needs rejoice in God through our Lord Jesus Christ." For Campbell a limited theory of the atonement could give no place to the assurance of faith. Such a theory would assure us only of the truth of God's word; the doctrine of assurance spoke rather of the truth of God's love. Campbell never tired of commending this view of God to his people. At the funeral of Isabella Campbell of Gareloch the rain fell heavily, and the funeral party was crowded into the cabin of the steamer on which they were traveling to the burial place. Campbell began to speak: "I feel it my duty to improve the time in saying something of what it has been my privilege to know of her whose remains we accompany." The mourners paused from their other conversations to listen. "Let me explain to you—the secret spring of all that distinguished her was the simplicity of the assurance of her faith. I press that faith on you." For an hour and a half Campbell quietly explained his views, until the boat stopped.

The Heresy Trial

Not all of Campbell's parishioners accepted their minister's theological views with equanimity. In March 1830 twelve of them presented to the presbytery a petition complaining of heresy. But a counterpetition had also been drawn up over the signatures of eighty householders and heads of families, who expressed "their undiminished attachment to Mr. Campbell as their pastor."

The evidence in the case was heard before the Presbytery of Dumbarton in February 1831. Two statements of Campbell's were quoted that had aroused the particular disapproval of his opponents: (1) "God loves every child of Adam with a love the measure of which is to be seen in the agonies of Christ." (2) The person who knows that Christ died for every child of Adam is the person who is in the

condition to say to every human being, "Let there be peace with you
—peace between you and your God."

In March the presbytery found the charges laid against Campbell
proven. The Synod of Glasgow and Ayr upheld the verdict of the
lower court. In the end Campbell made an appeal to the highest
court of the church, the General Assembly.

When his case came to be heard before the Assembly, Campbell
quoted both Scripture and the earlier creeds and confessions of the
church. To the accusation that he held and promulgated that assurance is of the essence of faith and that atonement is universal, Campbell argued that as he saw things no previous creeds of the church
had ever limited the extent of Christ's atonement. When the church
accepted the Confession of Faith, it did so with the declaration that
the Confession contained "nothing contrary to the received doctrine
of this Kirk." On the doctrine of assurance, with which he had been
charged, Campbell quoted from the Scots Confession of the Reformation period: "Everlasting death has had, and shall have, power and
dominion over all who have not been, are not, or shall not be reborn
from above. This rebirth is wrought by the power of the Holy Ghost
creating in the hearts of God's chosen ones an assured faith in the
promise of God revealed to us in his Word." On the doctrine of
universal atonement Campbell said: "I do teach that the atonement
was for the whole human race without exception or distinction."
Nevertheless, he did not hold the theory of universal restitution. He
believed in the universality of the atonement, but that in itself did
not imply that a single soul would be exempt from future misery.

In the course of the debate one of Campbell's antagonists refuted
his interpretation of the Confession of Faith: "We are far from appealing to the Word of God on this ground," he interjected. "It is by
the Confession of Faith that we must stand: by it we hold our livings."

Campbell summed up his own attitude to the Confession: "The
Church at no time has contained all the light that is in her living
Head. . . . If a Confession of Faith were something to stint and stop
the Church's growth in light and knowledge, and to say, 'Thus far
shalt thou go and no further,' then a Confession of Faith would be
the greatest curse that ever befell a Church."

The house was very still when Dr. Campbell, the father of the
accused, stood before his son's critics and supporters. "I bow to any
decision to which you may think it right to come. Moderator, I am
not afraid for my son; though his brethren cast him out, the Master
whom he serves will not forsake him; and while I live, I will never
be ashamed to be the father of so holy and blameless a son."

The time for debate on the issue ended. A decision had to be reached. Would the General Assembly agree with the lower courts that the doctrines of assurance as of the essence of faith and the universality of Christ's atonement and pardon were contrary to Scripture? What would be the Assembly's view of the relationship of the Westminster Confession of Faith to earlier creeds and confessions? And how much weight would be given to the Christlike character of the accused?

BIBLIOGRAPHY

The following materials were used in the preparation of this case and are recommended for further study.

Campbell, Donald. *Memorials of John McLeod Campbell.* London: Macmillan and Co., Ltd., 1877.
Campbell, John McLeod. *The Nature of the Atonement and Its Relation to Remission of Sins and Eternal Life.* 6th ed. London: Macmillan and Co., Ltd., 1906.
Drummond, Andrew L., and Bulloch, James. *The Scottish Church, 1688–1843: The Age of the Moderates.* Edinburgh: Saint Andrew Press, 1973.
Hanna, Thomas, ed. *Letters of Thomas Erskine of Linlathen.* Edinburgh: David Douglas, 1877.
Macleod, John. *Scottish Theology in Relation to Church History Since the Reformation.* Edinburgh: The Publications Committee of the Free Church of Scotland, 1943.
McCrie, C. G. *The Confessions of the Church of Scotland: Their Evolution and History.* Edinburgh: Macniven and Wallace, 1907.
Oliphant, Mrs. Margaret. *The Life of Edward Irving, Minister of the National Scotch Church.* Harper & Brothers, 1862.
Wright, Ronald Selby. *Fathers of the Kirk.* London: Oxford University Press, 1960.

12

Mary Baker Eddy vs. Joseph Cook
and A. J. Gordon (A.D. 1885)

Joseph Cook, Monday lecturer to the city's religious elite, doubted that good would come of Mrs. Mary Baker Eddy's "invasion" of Boston. He considered himself a "Scientific Christian," and he saw the new sect as anything but "Christian Science." Thus when the Rev. A. J. Gordon, an upstanding and sincere Baptist clergyman at the Clarendon Street Church, wrote a scathing attack on the movement and the "false salvation" it proffered, Cook determined to read the letter as a preface to his upcoming Monday lecture. He borrowed a copy of *Science and Health,* just to confirm for himself that what Gordon said was true. Then on February 23, 1885, he read Gordon's letter adding some personal words of rebuke in addition.

Mary Baker Eddy and her group of believers in Christian Science weighed several alternative reactions: Should they ignore the incident? Should they complain, or perhaps even sue the man for libel? Or should they ask for equal time to refute the charges?

A. J. Gordon

Born in 1836 in New Hampshire and graduated from Brown University in 1860, Adoniram Judson Gordon entered immediately the Newton Theological Seminary and was graduated three years later. He was for six years pastor of the Jamaica Plains Church, before being called from Boston's suburbs to become minister of the Clarendon Street Baptist Church in the city. From the time of his arrival in 1869, Gordon sought to make the church a place of Christian song as well

---

This case study was prepared by Professor Louis Weeks of the Louisville Presbyterian Theological Seminary as a basis for class discussion rather than to illustrate either effective or ineffective handling of a situation.

as the locus of good preaching.

When Dwight L. Moody, with his trusted friend and songleader Ira Sankey, came to "the Hub of the Universe" for a revival in 1877, Gordon was among those convicted and convinced in a protracted meeting. He saw the power of God moving to heal at least thirty drunkards during the time of Moody's sojourn in Boston. He witnessed the trainloads of people coming in chartered transportation from all over New England, and he counted attendance at the Tabernacle where over seventy thousand were present for one or more services. The Clarendon Street Church, less than a hundred yards from the huge tent, even received sometimes overflow crowds for the sessions of "inquiry." But what meant the most was personal for Gordon, and, as he later recounted, how the Spirit came upon him:

I simply knelt and said, "O God, Thou hast said by the lips of Jesus that Thou art more ready to give the Holy Spirit to them that ask Thee than we are to give good gifts to our children. Father, I take Thee at Thy word. I ask Thee in Jesus' name for the Holy Spirit."
Then I got up and went about my work.

To the question from a hearer, "Was that all?" Gordon replied, "What more is necessary?" He cooperated with Joseph Cook, and other ministers in the city, to increase the measure of Christian temperance regarding the use of liquor. He also led in the work of the Boston Industrial Temporary Home, a place where indigent and out-of-work people might find help.

But A. J. Gordon's chief theological convictions were that the Bible is an infallible book, that Christian life should ideally be missionary in its thrust, that Jesus calls people out of love of mammon to love of himself, and that the road to salvation is a narrow one. In his own words: "We can go on and outstrip the Word of God, but such advances are at our peril. Almost better to lag behind the truth than outrun it. Best of all is to walk in the truth."

Since Gordon believed a very Evangelical version of Christianity, he saw no reason for doubting that Jesus healed people in his own day and promised healing until he brought in the Kingdom. Indeed in 1882 he published a book, *The Ministry of Healing*. Nor did Gordon object to women in the ministry. In 1889, Gordon and his wife, Maria, would found the coeducational Boston Missionary Training School. Both men and women students were given field experience pastoring rural churches. In an article, "The Ministry of Women," published in 1894, Gordon would defend exegetically the full right of women to be ministers of the gospel. But Gordon perceived this

woman, Mary Baker Eddy, to be offering a fraudulent healing ministry. "It is a system of spiritual malpractice," he said in his letter; "and
is leading its subjects away from the simple faith of the gospel into
a vague and transcendental misbelief." His letter further labeled
Christian Science "an insidious delusion." "Its philosophy, briefly
stated, is this: Evil is not; sin, sickness, and death are unreal; 'matter
and the mortal body are nothing but a belief and illusion; there is
neither a personal Deity, a personal devil, nor a personal man.'"
Gordon compared these listed "tenets" of Christian Science with
specific Biblical texts to disprove them. He then called for Christians
to ignore the new gnosticism and to turn truly to Jesus for salvation.
It was this letter which Joseph Cook read.

Flavius Josephus Cook

Cook, born of early American Puritan stock in Ticonderoga, New
York, attended Phillips Academy, Yale, and Harvard, where he was
graduated in 1865. Following studies at Andover Theological Seminary, he traveled extensively in the Mid-East and attended various
European universities for two years. In 1874 he began to lead noon
prayer meetings in Boston's Tremont Temple on Mondays. By 1877,
the year Cook married, he had become exceedingly popular as the
leader of these services which now had become more lectures than
prayer meetings and which he always introduced with a pronouncement on current events. Both the introductions and the lectures
themselves were greeted with considerable "audience participation" in the form of voiced responses to his questions, applause, and
laughter at his jokes. A committee, which included the governor of
Massachusetts, prestigious clergy, businessmen, and Boston professionals, overseered the Monday Lectures at Tremont Temple and
supplied payment for Cook as well as published his weekly oration.
Cook's attention moved increasingly to focus on the relationship of
science and religion, as well as other topics of more transitory interest for Christian men (who comprised his audience). As collected in
book form, the topics included *Biology* (1877), *Transcendentalism*
(1877), *Orthodoxy* (1877), *Conscience* (1878), *Marriage* (1878), *Labor*
(1879), *Socialism* (1880), and *Occident* (1884). Characteristically, he
offered a rather open, but not too radical, discussion of each subject.
He summarized the views of experts and offered a mainstream opinion on the topic. His resolution of the issue was usually one with
which his audience could agree as being of "good sense."
For example, Cook declared boldly that the latest advances of
science buttressed orthodox Christian doctrine. At least four of the

lectures transcribed in *Biology* addressed the evidences for life after death. And in *Orthodoxy,* he outlined some others of his cardinal doctrines. "Is there nothing in God to fear?" he asked; and he answered himself that "God cannot be an enswathing kiss, without being also a consuming fire." Indeed, the person "who is unholy long enough will be unholy longer." Therefore it was sensible to see that God, while ultimately benevolent, must also be seen as just and unswervingly righteous.

Along with a continuing accent on the "wrath of God," now redefined as human "remoteness from God," Cook proclaimed the practical truth of the doctrine of "Trinity." He said that the doctrine had "always been held by Orthodoxy for its practical value." He claimed that the doctrine "brought in the organizing and redemptive idea of God's fatherhood, and especially the communion of men with God as personal."

Again, he saw the "Atonement" as necessary amid Christian beliefs, but he did not seek rigidity in specifying the way in which Christ worked to redeem people. In a lecture on atonement, he quoted considerable portions of *Macbeth* to his audience as an illustration of human nature and the need for Jesus' work. The atonement was substitutionary, according to Cook; but he distinguished between the punishment and the chastisement. Jesus did not receive personal demerit, he said, but rather received the pain of humanity:

> If religious science will begin the fashion, and never use a term of importance without defining it, I for one will try to keep step. . . . The chastisement of our offences was laid upon our Lord. It is nowhere presumed in the Scriptures that personal demerit can be transferred from individuality to individuality.

Cook began and ended with Christian mainstream orthodoxy, and thus he naturally disapproved of Mrs. Eddy's claiming special truth for her "re-discovered" way of Scientific Christianity. Since he cooperated with Gordon, and knew the man personally, he respected the Baptist's opinion of the "insidious delusion" and accordingly read the letter.

Mary Baker Eddy

Born on July 16, 1821, to farming parents in Bow, New Hampshire, Mary Baker grew up the youngest child in the family. Her father, an orthodox Congregationalist, was strict in familial authoritarianism and theological Calvinism alike. She married in 1843, and moved south with her husband George Washington Glover. However, his untimely death in Wilmington, North Carolina, six months later left her pregnant, widowed, and neurotically depressed. Her son, also named George, although born when Mary returned to her family in New Hampshire, was given to Mahala Sanborn for wet-nursing; and he stayed with her even when his mother married and moved to Minnesota.

For her part, Mary sought various popular "cures" for her poor health, indulged in voracious reading, and published infrequent pieces of verse. In 1853, she married Dr. Daniel Patterson. In her new home in Franklin, New Hampshire, she became virtually bedridden, and continued taking morphine to relieve her neuralgia and loneliness. In 1862, Patterson, on one of his periodic peregrinations as an itinerant dentist, was sent south by the Union and captured by the Confederates. Mary entered a course of hydrotherapy in nearby Hill. The water cure failed, but the rumor mill there produced word of Dr. Phineas Parkhurst Quimby, another healer. She went to Portland, Maine, to seek his therapy.

Quimby had employed first mesmerism and then hypnosis to effect healing. Subsequently he had developed a Christian healing process, and a philosophical idealism as a theoretical buttress. Healing, according to Quimby, was a mental process. He described his work as a Christian endeavor also. Jesus Christ was a dualistic person, said Quimby. "He had no false belief," and Jesus was thus the embodied ideal of the Christ. He could heal persons even though they were physically absent from him. Therefore the process was necessarily spiritual-mental. It was accomplished through Jesus' mental power, and he took their "disease," or afflictions of falseness, on himself. This was a Christian process, given by Jesus to believers to be employed. And Quimby used it, with great initial success in the case of Mrs. Patterson.

Gradually Mrs. Patterson, for four years reunited with her sometimes present husband upon his release from prison, undertook to explain Quimby's method to various groups of people. Occasionally she worked as a healer herself. In early 1866, however, Quimby died and Mary Patterson slipped on the ice, hurting her back. According to her later reports of the incident, the attending physician gave her no hope of living.

It was in this desperate plight, deserted by her husband and with the homeopathic physician giving up, that Mary Patterson claimed to have discovered Christian Science. Though intermittently plagued by personal pain and despair (she soon wrote to another Quimby disciple, J. A. Dresser, for help), she prayed and read Scripture to find health. And she thenceforth devoted herself to proclaiming Christian Science. For at least ten years she worked feverishly on "the Book" and traveled from home to home among her acquaintances and temporary disciples.

She entered into one arrangement with Richard Kennedy in Lynn, Massachusetts, under which Dr. Kennedy would practice medicine and she would teach her course of study in healing. Evidently the two practitioners in healing and teaching achieved some degree of popularity, for records show that a number of persons received their services. By 1872, however, the partnership was dissolved because, among other arenas of incompatibility, Kennedy proved to be a "manipulationist." Mrs. Patterson, still legally married until 1873, eschewed the rubbing of a patient's body for spiritual healing—even if only the head and solar plexus as Kennedy did. It debased the spiritual to resort to "physical" contact as a device. The fight to divide the practice was a bitter one.

It was in this dilemma that Mrs. Patterson began speaking of malicious animal magnetism, or, cryptically, "M.A.M." She said mental powers of people included the peculiar influence that one person was capable of holding over another. Like mesmerism, or hypnosis, it was a mental process; but its nature was more broadly defined, and later she labeled it a form of "carnal enmity" against God. As over against this negative power, the Christian Scientist participated in ideal, spiritual power—and grew in perfect love.

Another discouraging quarrel, in addition to the Kennedy affair, erupted with Mary's second male assistant—Daniel H. Spofford. She published a book she called *Science and Health,* and Spofford agreed to market the work for her. It contained 456 pages, covering such subjects as "Natural Science," "Imposition and Demonstration," and "Spirit and Matter." In it, she claimed that people, as spiritual beings, have no death because Jesus promised life on account of his life. She said that God is the healer, and the New Testament practice of healing had now been rediscovered. She taught that there is only essentially the Spirit, and that people in a primitive condition misperceived the world to contain a devil. There could be none really because God is good, and made everything "good." And she declared that all real life is in the Spirit—never in matter itself. In the Preface, she maintained:

The science of man alone can make him harmonious, unfold his utmost possibilities, and establish the perfection of man. To admit God the Principle of all being, and live in accordance with this Principle, is the Science of Life, but to reproduce the harmony of being, errors of personal sense must be destroyed, even as the science of music must correct tones caught from the ear, to give the sweet concord of sound. There are many theories of physic, and theology; and many calls in each of their directions for the right way; but we propose to settle the question of "What is Truth?" on the ground of proof. Let that method of healing the sick and establishing Christianity be adopted that is found to give the most health, and make the best Christians, and you will then give science a fair field; in which case we are assured of its triumph over all opinions and beliefs. Sickness and sin have ever had their doctors, but the question is, have they become less because of them?

Spofford argued against her revising the book once printed, in the interest of selling the available. She felt, on the contrary, that new truths were being revealed to her and should be included in a second edition of *Science and Health.* Spofford may also have felt himself gradually displaced, as Mary Glover (regaining the name of her first husband upon divorcing the second) depended increasingly upon Asa Gilbert Eddy, who had been healed by her and studied under her. Eddy assumed increasing responsibility within the small coterie of believers, and in a Unitarian ceremony Mrs. Glover married Mr. Eddy, January 1, 1877. Spofford, acting from whatever motive(s), closed out the book at a cut price. This sell-off left Mrs. Eddy without the means for publishing a revision. To top it all off, he began teaching doctrines of healing that were contradictory to Mrs. Eddy's, and he accused her of being ineffectual, if not downright harmful, to the persons she sought to heal.

One of Mrs. Eddy's loyal students, Lucretia Brown of Ipswich, Massachusetts, accused Spofford of causing her "great suffering of body and mind and severe spinal pains and neuralgia." Spofford was judged innocent in the trial, which was soon labeled the Ipswich Witchcraft Case. Other suits, brought by students and patients, accused Mrs. Eddy of confusing them with diverse teaching, and of exacting work from them without paying promised salary for it. Although she was also exonerated in the processes, the sect was threatened with dissolution by splintering.

Trouble was compounded when her new husband, Mr. Eddy, and an associate were arrested for the murder of Spofford in October 1878. Spofford turned up hale and hearty, but the accusing officers temporarily charged the men with a "conspiracy" to commit the act anyhow. As if these trials were not sufficient, Job-like Mrs. Eddy was greeted with an atrocious printing of the second version of *Science and Health,* the revision on which she pinned so much promise. She had the first volume immediately withdrawn, and also the second after only a few were sold.

To cap the cluster of misfortunes, on October 21, 1881, eight of her best students walked out en masse, accusing her of obstreperous behavior and hypocrisy. Crestfallen, Mrs. Eddy was ordained pastor by the remainder—her faithful remnant. She led the group from Lynn to Boston, and founded the Massachusetts Metaphysical College. She also brought out a third edition of *Science and Health,* which seemed vastly improved over the other two. Sadly, her husband died shortly after the move to Boston, but Mrs. Eddy's work now showed signs of prospering. Many of her patients and students were young women, who, when convinced of her greatness, felt called to spread the gospel of Christian Science. Thus the growing effect of the movement was felt even among the businessmen, politicians, and men of culture who gathered in Tremont Temple each Monday to listen approvingly to Cook.

These social and business leaders would scarcely change their attitudes if Mrs. Eddy addressed them. Their condescension was disturbing, but so was the blatant attack on the new movement. And the task of the minister was to present the truth. Christian Science seemed on the verge of success, and the forum would be a good one from which to speak.

AN EPILOGUE

Mrs. Eddy decided to take the opportunity to speak. She decided to take this chance to expound the major points in Christian Science and to dispel the misunderstanding.

Cook "graciously" allowed Mrs. Eddy ten minutes on the Monday, March 16, program. She took the floor, faced the audience of men, and issued her rebuttal:

> As the time so kindly allotted me is insufficient for even a synopsis of Christian Science, I shall confine myself to questions and answers.
>
> Am I a spiritualist?
>
> I am not, and never was. I understand the impossibility of intercommunion between the so-called dead and living. There have always attended my life phenomena of an uncommon order, which spiritualists have miscalled mediumship; but I clearly understand that no human agencies were employed,—that the divine Mind reveals itself to humanity through spiritual law. And to such as are "waiting for the adoption, to wit, the redemption of our body." Christian Science reveals the infinitude of divinity

and the way of man's salvation from sickness and death, as wrought out by Jesus, who robbed the grave of victory and death of its sting. I understand that God is an ever-present help in all times of trouble,—have found Him so; and would have no other gods, no remedies in drugs, no material medicine.

Do I believe in a personal God?

I believe in God as the Supreme Being. I know not what the person of omnipotence and omnipresence is, or what the infinite includes; therefore, I worship that of which I can conceive, first, as a loving Father and Mother; then, as thought ascends the scale of being to diviner consciousness, God becomes to me, as to the apostle who declared it, "God is Love,"—divine Principle,— which I worship; and "after the manner of my fathers, so worship I God."

Do I believe in the atonement of Christ?

I do; and this atonement becomes more to me since it includes man's redemption from sickness as well as from sin. I reverence and adore Christ as never before.

It brings to my sense, and to the sense of all who entertain this understanding of the Science of God, a whole salvation.

How is the healing done in Christian Science?

This answer includes too much to give you any conclusive idea in a brief explanation. I can name some means by which it is not done.

It is not one mind acting upon another mind; it is not the transference of human images of thought to other minds; it is not supported by the evidence before the personal senses,—Science contradicts this evidence; it is not of the flesh, but of the Spirit. It is Christ come to destroy the power of the flesh; it is Truth over error; that understood, gives man ability to rise above the evidence of the senses, take hold of the eternal energies of Truth, and destroy mortal discord with immortal harmony,—the grand verities of being. It is not one mortal thought transmitted to another's thought from the human mind that holds within itself all evil.

Our Master said of one of his students, "He is a devil," and repudiated the idea of casting out devils through Beelzebub. Erring human mind is by no means a desirable or efficacious healer. Such suppositional healing I deprecate. It is in no way allied to divine power. All human control is animal magnetism, more despicable than all other methods of treating disease.

Christian Science is not a remedy of faith alone, but combines faith with understanding, through which we may touch the hem of His garment; and know that omnipotence has all power. "I am the Lord, and there is none else, there is no God beside me."

Is there a personal man?

The Scriptures inform us that man was made in the image and likeness of God. I commend the Icelandic translation: "He created man in the image and likeness of Mind, in the image and likeness of Mind created He him." To my sense, we have not seen all man; he is more than personal sense can cognize, who is the image and likeness of the infinite. I have not seen a perfect man in mind or body,—and such must be the personality of him who is the true likeness: the lost image is not this personality, and corporeal man is this lost image, hence, it doth not appear what is the real personality of man. The only cause for making this question of personality a point, or of any importance, is that man's perfect model should be held in mind, whereby to improve his present condition; that his contemplation regarding himself should turn away from inharmony, sickness, and sin, to that which is the image of his Maker.

Confrontation with the mainstream on matters of belief, faith, and life did not always characterize Mrs. Eddy. But this time she had spoken. The burden of proof now lay on Cook, Gordon, and the other representatives of middle Protestantism. In what respects should they accept her statements, or reject them, in matters of doctrine? How might they react? How should they react?

BIBLIOGRAPHY

The following materials were used in the preparation of this case and are recommended for further study.

Dictionary of American Biography. Vol. VI. Charles Scribner's Sons, 1943.

Eddy, Mary Baker. *Miscellaneous Writings (1883–1896).* Trustees of Mary Baker Eddy. Bjoston, 1896.

Gottschalk, Stephen. *The Emergence of Christian Science in American Religious Life.* University of California Press, 1973.

James, Edward., ed. *Notable American Women.* Harvard University Press, 1971.

Peel, Robert. *Mary Baker Eddy; The Years of Discovery.* Holt, Rinehart & Winston, Inc., 1966.

———. *Mary Baker Eddy: The Years of Trial.* Holt, Rinehart & Winston, Inc., 1971.

13
Christus Victor (A.D. 1930)

In the spring of 1930, Gustaf Aulén, then professor of systematic theology in the University of Lund, delivered the Olaus Petri Lectures at the University of Uppsala. An English version of the lectures was produced by A. G. Hebert and published in 1931 under the title *Christus Victor*. Reflecting in 1950 on what happened in theology during the generation that followed his lectures, Aulén said that he saw no reason to change his outlook:

> Some years ago I wrote a little book about the Atonement, called in the English translation *Christus Victor*. Then I spoke about three different views of the Atonement, described as the "classic," the "Latin," and the "subjective" views. . . . It was my intention to emphasize that the outlook of the Atonement as a drama, where the love of God in Christ fights and conquers the hostile powers, is a central and decisive perspective which never can be omitted and which indeed must stamp every really Christian doctrine of the Atonement. Since that time nothing has happened in theology which has induced me to change this opinion. On the contrary, I am more than ever convinced that without this outlook of the Atonement as a drama one will lose connection with the fundamental biblical message.

Ten years later, a Canadian theologian who was critical of Aulén's lectures conceded that "for the past three decades they have played a considerable part in discussions of soteriology."

This case study was prepared by Professor Ross Mackenzie of Union Theological Seminary in Virginia as a basis for class discussion rather than to illustrate either effective or ineffective handling of a situation.

The Atonement in Later Lutheranism

After the years of Luther's ascendancy the emphasis among his followers increasingly fell on the formulation of pure doctrine. But the period after the Reformer's death was marked by intensely sharp differences, and the *rabies theologorum,* or "madness of the theologians," divided Lutheran from Lutheran.

The general view of the atonement held by Lutheran dogmaticians in the sixteenth and seventeenth centuries was that of a balancing between God's punitive justice and his mercy, a *temperamentum misericordiae et justitiae.* Later Lutheran confessions also expressed a strong antipathy toward the Socinian error, as many of the theologians regarded it, that "redemption" in Scripture was simply a metaphor for deliverance. Since God is judge, they taught, divine justice demanded some balance between his mercy and his justice. Thus the Lutheran teachers tended to return to the Anselmian doctrine of an absolutely necessary satisfaction.

Martin Chemnitz, the leading spirit in writing the Formula of Concord, argued that because human nature after the Fall was subject to the wrath of God and damnation, it was necessary that the Mediator make satisfaction for us in his human nature. "For the wrath of God cannot be appeased by human satisfaction or human powers," he said, "nor can death be destroyed and life restored. For this is a work of divine power."

Among other Lutheran scholars of the eighteenth century, however, such views were not acceptable. Johann Salomo Semler held that the early Christian teachers, minting a language with which to express what God had done in Christ for human salvation, inevitably used the metaphors of sacrifice. "These old expressions and idioms," he said, "now receive an even greater content when the Christian uses them." The key to this greater content was to see how the New Testament writers used the sacrificial language and ideas of the Old Testament. There was one important difference. The sacrifice of Jesus was not merely one more death in a sequence of sacrifices, but the perfect sacrifice, offered once and for all. In Semler's analysis of the atonement the crucial theologian was Anselm, whose doctrine of the atonement had so strongly influenced the ideas of atonement in Lutheran orthodoxy. But Semler subjected Anselm's views to a thorough revision: to say that Christ received in his own death the punishment due to our sins is to say that God deals graciously with us. Christ has suffered, not to appease the divine wrath, but with the ultimate purpose of reforming our character.

In Anselm's *Cur Deus homo* the doctrine of substitutionary atonement had been given a central place, and until the period of the
Enlightenment the doctrine of the atonement had been understood
in Lutheran orthodoxy largely in terms of substitution. But the in-
dividualism and rationalism of the Enlightenment made it harder for
theologians to accept that any person could assume punishment for
another. A more direct question came into the center of the theological debate: How could a God of love be satisfied with the sufferings
of an innocent Christ to atone for the sins of the world?

In his study of Protestant theology from Rousseau to Ritschl, Karl
Barth observed that in Königsberg, where he lived near the castle
which also served as a prison, Immanuel Kant was angered by the
loud and persistent hymn singing of the prisoners. It was particularly
irksome to him in the summer, when he liked to philosophize with
his windows open, and he complained to the town president about
the "stentorian devotions of those hypocrites in the gaol." Barth had
been arguing that Kant denied the validity of all expiations which
sought to replace a change of heart as the true and decisive but also
at the same time nonintuitive human need, whether these expiations
were of the atoning or of the sacramental kind.

Kant, according to Barth, had rejected the "vicarious ideal" of
Christ. Liberal Protestantism in the nineteenth century tended likewise to be detached and critical in its attitude toward dogmas such
as the atonement. Yet Albrecht Ritschl, who was regarded by many
as the founder of the liberal Protestant school, did not want merely
to reduce Christianity to whatever the secular critics of the age could
swallow, but sought rather to maintain the Christian truth in its
integrity. Ritschl elaborated his views on the atonement in three
large volumes which appeared between 1870 and 1874 under the
title *Die christliche Lehre von der Rechtfertigung und Versöhnung.*
In a typical passage he wrote thus of justification as adoption by God:

> The title of Judge as applied to God has therefore for Christians
> no real place alongside of, or over, the relation in which he
> stands to them as Father. It is only, therefore, when the love of
> God, regarded as Father, is conceived as the will which works
> toward the destined end, that the real equivalence of forgive-
> ness and justification, which is represented in the religious con-
> ception of things, can be made good. If, however, God be pre-
> conceived as Judge in the forensic sense, the two ideas come into
> direct antagonism with one another, as was indeed explicitly
> maintained by representatives of the older theology. The man
> who has gone through the punishment he has merited can, of
> course, be no more looked upon as a criminal, but he cannot by

any means yet be regarded as an active and successful member of the moral community; in order to attain this place, the discharged culprit must give special evidence of his fitness for membership in the community. If, therefore, a judicial procedure on the part of God is recognised in this, that he regards sinners as free from punishment and guilt on account of the satisfaction which Christ has made, he must also, in order to judge them as positively righteous, impute to them the merit of Christ.

The Leading Ideas of Christus Victor

In his preface to the 1931 edition of *Christus Victor*, the translator, A. G. Hebert, stated that the important and original contribution of the book was its strong delineation of the view that sets the incarnation in direct connection with the atonement, and proclaims that it is God himself who in Christ has delivered humankind from the power of evil. This was the patristic teaching; it dominated the New Testament; and it had therefore every right to be called the typically Christian view, or, in Aulén's phrase, the "classic" idea of the atonement. In Aulén's thinking, Hebert went on, this idea was to be distinguished from the view that grew up in the West on the basis of the forensic idea of sin as transgression of law and received its first clear formulation from Anselm. That view regarded the atonement as not in the full sense God's work, but rather as the act whereby "man in Christ makes reparation for man's sin."

In his own description, Aulén depicted the central theme of the "classic" idea of the atonement as a divine conflict and victory: Christ —Christus Victor—fights against and triumphs over the evil powers of the world, the "tyrants" under which human beings are in bondage and suffering. In Christ, God reconciles the world to himself. The most marked difference between the classical or "dramatic" type and the so-called "objective" or Anselmian type lies in the fact that it represents the work of atonement or reconciliation as from first to last a work of God himself, a *continuous* divine work; whereas according to the other view the act of atonement has indeed its origin in God's will, but is, in its carrying out, an offering made to God by Christ "as man and on man's behalf," and may therefore be called a *discontinuous* divine work.

The Latin theory of the atonement first appeared fully developed in the *Cur Deus homo*—a book, Aulén said, which has been so universally regarded as the typical expression of the Latin theory that this theory has commonly been known as the Anselmian doctrine. The

Latin idea of penance provided sufficient explanation of the Latin doctrine of the atonement. Its root idea was that human beings must make an offering or payment to satisfy God's justice:

> Two points immediately emerge: First, that the whole idea is essentially legalistic; and second, that, in speaking of Christ's work, the emphasis is all laid on that which is done by Christ *as man* in relation to God. It is a wholly different outlook from that of the classic idea which we have hitherto been studying.

From the historical perspective, however, the Latin type of atonement turns out to be really a sidetrack in the history of Christian dogma—admittedly of vast importance and influence, but still only a sidetrack.

The main line in the development of doctrine was continued, not by Anselm and the medieval Scholastics, but by Luther. Ritschl misunderstood Luther in ascribing his teaching on the atonement to the same juridical type as Anselm's. Yet the decisive proof that there is no continuity of tradition between Anselm, Luther, and Lutheran orthodoxy is summed up in the following three points:

> First, in those places where it is altogether necessary for him to express himself with the greatest possible care and the greatest possible exactness, as, for instance, in the Catechisms, he always returns to the dramatic idea.
>
> Second, he himself repeatedly assures us, with all possible clearness, that the statements of the meaning of the atonement in dramatic terms give the very essence of the Christian faith; they are *capitalia nostrae theologiae* (the chief points of our theology).
>
> Third, and chiefly, the dramatic view of the work of Christ stands in organic relation with his theological outlook as a whole.

Therefore, Aulén concludes, Luther stands out in the history of Christian doctrine as the one who expressed the classic idea of the atonement with greater power than any before him. From the sideline of the Latin theory he bends right back to the main line, making a direct connection with the New Testament and patristic teaching.

Gustaf Aulén and "Lundensian Theology"

In 1901, Nathan Söderblom came to the University of Uppsala as professor with a distinguished reputation in the study of comparative religion. His own theological beliefs had been influenced by Albrecht Ritschl and other representatives of liberal Protestantism, and accordingly his outlook was suspect in the eyes of some of the defenders of the older orthodoxy. Serving under him as docent, or lecturer, from 1907 to 1913 was Gustaf Aulén. Another colleague on the faculty was Einar Billing, who was appointed professor of systematic theology in 1909.

In Sweden the history of dogma and the history of ideas belong to systematic theology, not to church history. Systematic theology has consequently had a strong historical emphasis, and the investigation of the history of Christian thought has customarily been undertaken by systematic theologians. Both Söderblom and Billing directed their attention to the distinctiveness of the Biblical faith in God. Every religion presents a definite inner unity in terms of a fundamental motif around which the faith of the religious community is organized. The fundamental motif of the Christian faith is the concept of the God who acts, and whose place of activity is the external world. In defining the meaning of Biblical faith in this fashion, Söderblom and Billing faced increasing criticism not only from contemporary Lutheran orthodoxy but from the advocates of a rationalistic and liberal Protestantism.

In 1913, Aulén was appointed professor of systematic theology in the University of Lund, the same year in which Edvard Lehmann came from Berlin to that university as professor of comparative religion. Lehmann's docent was Anders Nygren. A revival of theology began at Lund around 1920 when Aulén and Nygren entered into their fruitful collaboration; and in the "Lundensian Theology," much of what had been initiated at Uppsala at the beginning of the century was rediscovered. Aulén came to be generally acknowledged as "the developer par excellence of the Lundensian theology," the one through whom the influence of Söderblom came to be felt, and who succeeded in bridging the earlier work at Uppsala with the revival at Lund.

The independent line of thought that was specifically Aulén's own began in the interest which Söderblom and Billing had taken in the unique position which the Biblical faith in God occupies in comparative religion. With this starting point Aulén attempted to sketch the fundamental motif of the Christian faith from the New Testament up to the sixteenth century, and so to relate Christian faith to other conceptions which appear in the history of ideas, Platonism and juridical thought forms in particular. As a consequence Aulén devoted much of his thinking to the question of dividing the history of dogma into periods. The critical issue for him was to determine what difference each period of time had made in clarifying or obscuring the Christian faith. There have been times when the Christian faith was overshadowed by juridical ways of thinking or Platonic ideas, but there have been other times when it has emerged from these distortions and its original splendor has been renewed. There was a unity, Aulén held, that linked the New Testament, the early church, and the Lutheran Reformation, whereas the Middle Ages and the post-Reformation period were periods of eclipse.

It was characteristic of the Lundensian theology that Aulén and Nygren devoted most of their scholarly life to studying the thought of the early church. Both of them regarded Luther as a restorer of what was original in early Christianity and the primitive church. Hence Luther is to be understood as a theologian for the whole church, a restorer of what is truly catholic, in contrast to the deviations of the Middle Ages.

Nygren's own successor at Lund, Gustaf Wingren, summarized the shift in direction which Swedish theology had taken in the twentieth century:

> When Swedish theology has dealt with the relationship between Luther and Lutheranism, it has almost always concerned itself with the *difference* between these two, and in particular it has emphasised the similarity between medieval scholasticism and Lutheran orthodoxy. Luther is isolated, and regarded as pretty well unique in his biblical purity—and it is for this reason that he is able to speak to us in the present day. Söderblom, whose thinking is marked by a greater multiformity and at times eclecticism, gives no support to isolating Luther like this. But it is with Einar Billing that this thoroughly Swedish concentration on Luther, or rather, on the Bible and Luther, can be said to begin.
> . . . It is characteristic in Sweden that it is the *Lutheran* scholars (and in particular Nygren and Aulén) who have devoted most of their time to studying the thought-world of the primitive church. The early church and the Reformation are seen in Swedish theology to be essentially one. Both are regarded as true and normative interpretations of biblical Christianity, a fact which gives the whole of Swedish theology a markedly *ecumenical* basis.

Responses to Christus Victor: *Approval, Questions, and Criticism*

From its first appearance Aulén's little book, in the words of Eugene R. Fairweather, "played a considerable part in discussions of soteriology." Its central argument was strongly endorsed by many. Among those who approved Aulén's thesis the following comments were typical: The New Testament *does* speak of the work of Christ in terms of conflict and victory. To insist that the atonement from first to last is the act of God and not of man is a necessary stress. There is a sound basis for pointing out weaknesses in the Anselmian theory. In traditional understandings of the atonement this idea of Christus Victor has been slighted.

An American theologian of Swedish origins, Nels F. S. Ferré, spoke of Aulén as "conclusively the theologian of God's divine love in Christ. Not to take Aulén seriously here," he asserted, "is to miss the mid-point of all his theology." According to Ferré, Aulén illustrates God as agape by the work of Christ in redemption:

> Here once again Aulén resorts to the historical method. The use of history to uncover Christian doctrine is with Aulén almost on a par with his main stress on the systematic exposition of it. Aulén finds that the main motif of the New Testament and the Fathers was the *coram deo* rather than the *coram hominibus,* or from God to man rather than from man to God.

Others, while expressing appreciation to Aulén for his insights, raised questions which they said had not been removed by advocacy of the "dramatic" view of the atonement. Could any one view be regarded as "classic"? In the "classical motif" of the Christian faith God himself was the subject of the atonement. How was this to be related to the emerging sense among numbers of Catholic and Protestant theologians that it is appropriate and even necessary today for theology to begin with anthropology? And granted that there are weaknesses in the Anselmian view of satisfaction, did it not also express a distinct and genuinely Biblical view?

Among those who differed with Aulén, two criticisms in particular were made: first, his evaluation of Anselm was judged to be incomplete and unfair; and second, he went astray in asserting that the dramatic theory was the only one that Luther propounded.

Aulén, it was said, rejected the "satisfaction" theory of Anselm, according to which man through Christ makes satisfaction for his sin to God and thereby gains salvation. But is such an interpretation of Anselm either complete or fair? In an essay written in 1948, F. W. Camfield asked whether all that happened in the "classic" idea was that militaristic and strategical metaphors came to take the place of juristic and forensic. "What especially concerns us," he said, "is that we are presented from the evangelical side with a view of the atonement which has absolutely renounced the idea of substitution." How could victory over evil as a *power* be atonement for evil as a *guilt?*

Another criticism of Aulén came from Ted Peters. Aulén, according to Peters, alleged that Anselm's doctrine of satisfaction depended on a legalistic structuring of the relationship between God and ourselves. But what Aulén has missed, and what should be obvious, is the Platonic structure behind Anselm's argument. There is one final reality for Anselm, God:

> Anselm supplies two answers why God ought not freely to forgive man's sin. First, such forgiveness would unjustly place the disobedient will on the same plane as the obedient one. The disobedient will would then become God-like, for only God's will is subject to the law or judgment of no one. (*Cur Deus homo*, I, 12.) Second, such forgiveness would do nothing to correct the disturbance of the order and beauty of the universe caused by sin. The slightest uncorrected disorder argues a deficiency either in God's justice or in his power, which is impossible if one affirms that God is deficient in neither. (*Ibid.*, I, 15.)

One sentence in *Christus Victor* made Peters ask if Aulén was not opening himself up to the charge of monotheletism if not monophysitism. Aulén had written: "The contrast between Anselm and the Fathers is as plain as daylight. They show how God became incarnate that he might redeem; he shows a human work of satisfaction, accomplished by Christ." Peters responded:

> It is becoming clear that the criterion by which Aulén assesses the various theories of the atonement is dependent on his own particular understanding of the incarnation and its purpose. For Aulén the redemptive purpose was achieved only because the acts of the incarnate one were really acts of God, in a sense which absolutely excludes the thought of any atoning work from man's side.
> ... Aulén is rendering a distortion of Anselm's view when he separates the incarnation from the atonement by asserting that satisfaction is simply man's task.

To Canadian critic Eugene R. Fairweather it seemed clear that Aulén's appeal to the historic catholic Christology against the "Latin" theology of redemption must be dismissed. He asked whether it was not Anselm's doctrine, rather than Aulén's critique, that was really at one with the Chalcedonian Christology as fully articulated in the fight against monotheletism. The duality in Anselm's teaching faithfully reflected the ideas of the church fathers, and it was no less compatible in his thought than in theirs with the ultimate unity of Christ's person and work. Not everyone was happy with the juridical language of Anselm's argument. The fact remained that his Christological presuppositions, with which his doctrine of the atonement was fully consistent, conformed strictly to the patristic teaching: "When Anselm so consistently and searchingly expounds the essence of man's redemption as a divine-human work, it is this patristic and conciliar vision of the divine humility in the incarnation that dominates his thinking." Fairweather concluded his criticism of Aulén by citing his own "Introduction to Anselm of Canterbury" in *A Scholastic Miscellany:*

> From start to finish the argument is dominated by the action of God—of God who made man, of God who was made man to offer, in manhood, an acceptable satisfaction to the divine nature. There is duality, of course, in the sense that the satisfaction required and made is a human act, but there is an underlying unity in the fact that it is God's omnipotent love that makes an acceptable human act possible. Anselm is concerned at once to stress the truth that God alone can be man's Redeemer, and to show the real significance of his taking human nature and dying a human death.

The other criticism directed against Aulén was that he had taken one motif in Luther's theology and attempted to superimpose it upon all the rest of the Reformer's thought. It was conceded that Aulén was probably correct in attributing an essential role to the Christus Victor theory of the atonement in Luther's thought. Luther's writings are full of accounts of Christ's conflict with the tyrannical powers of sin, death, and the devil. Aulén was also correct in contending that this interpretation of the atonement was originally related to the Reformer's doctrine of justification by faith. But Luther was not a theologian of one note, and Aulén went astray, it was said, in holding that the Christus Victor theory was the only one that Luther propounded. According to Peters, Luther also held a satisfaction perspective with regard to the work of Christ, and it has certain vital elements in common with Anselm: "Aulén has been insensitive," Peters said, "to the breadth and complex texture of Luther's many-sided theology." As an example of what he meant and in particular of the "near-organic relationship" between the notions of Christ's victory and satisfaction rendered to God, Peters cited Luther's Large Catechism:

> He has snatched us, poor lost creatures, from the jaws of hell, won us, made us free, and restored us to the Father's favor and grace. . . . The remaining parts of the article simply serve to clarify and express how and by what means this redemption was accomplished—that is, how much it cost Christ and what he paid and risked in order to bring us under his dominion. That is to say . . . he suffered, died, and was buried that he might make satisfaction for me and pay what I owed, not with silver and gold, but with his own precious blood.

Aulén on His Theological Theories

In his reflections in 1950 on what had happened in theology since his lectures were first published, Aulén admitted that all theological theories were only attempts tentatively to express what human language could never be able fully to express. However, there were in conclusion some points that he wanted now more strongly to emphasize:

> First, the universal and cosmic character of the great drama that has its center in the Atonement; secondly, the indissoluble connection between the cross and resurrection of Christ; and thirdly, that the Atonement is not only a work that is once for all completed but also a work that is continued until the last judgment, the church of Christ being the instrument of this work.

The issues had been posed, but not resolved; and there were persuasive voices saying that Aulén's appeal to the historic catholic Christology against the "Latin" theology of redemption must be dismissed. Who had the better arguments, Aulén or his critics? Which view or views of the atonement most nearly reflected the data of Scripture, the thought of the early church, and the position of Luther?

BIBLIOGRAPHY

The following materials were used in the preparation of this case and are recommended for further study.

Arden, G. Everett. "Swedish Theology," in *The Encyclopedia of the Lutheran Church*. Edited by Julius Bodensieck. Vol. 3, pp. 2305–2311. Augsburg Publishing House, 1965.

Aulén, Gustaf. *Christus Victor.* Translated by A. G. Hebert. The Macmillan Company, 1931.

Carlson, Edgar M. *The Reinterpretation of Luther.* The Westminster Press, 1948.

Fairweather, Eugene R. "Incarnation and Atonement: An Anselmian Response to Aulén's *Christus Victor,*" *Canadian Journal of Theology,* Vol. 7, No. 3 (July 1961), pp. 167–175.

Ferré, Nels F. S. *Swedish Contributions to Modern Theology, With Special Reference to Lundensian Thought.* Harper & Brothers, 1939.

————. "Theologians of Our Time. IX. The Theology of Gustaf Aulén," in *Expository Times*, Vol. 74, No. 11 (August 1963), pp. 324–327.

Horton, Walter M. *Contemporary Continental Theology. An Interpretation for Anglo-Saxons.* Harper & Brothers, 1938.

Peters, Ted. "The Atonement in Anselm and Luther, Second Thoughts About Gustaf Aulén's *Christus Victor,*" in *Lutheran Quarterly*, Vol. 24, No. 3 (August 1972), pp. 301–314.

Schilling, S. Paul. *Contemporary Continental Theologians.* Abingdon Press, 1966.

Wingren, Gustaf. *Theology in Conflict.* Translated by E. H. Wahlstrom. Muhlenberg Press, Publishers, 1958.

Part III

THE PERSON AND WORK OF CHRIST

Contemporary Understandings and Applications

14

Kimbanguist Membership in the World Council of Churches (A.D. 1968)

The application of the "Church of Jesus Christ on Earth Through the Prophet Simon Kimbangu" lay before the members of the Central Committee of the World Council of Churches. The Kimbanguist communion applied for membership expressly because they believed that their participation with Christian bodies on a global basis would fulfill prophecy made by the prophet himself. "In a moment of messianic inspiration," according to Henry Crane, a member of the staff of the World Student Christian Federation and a former missionary in the Congo, Kimbangu himself had foreseen that "Christians of all races would come from the ends of the earth to worship with them." Joseph Diangienda, spiritual head of the Kimbanguists and son of Simon Kimbangu himself, had signed the application and presented it to the committee in June 1968. The next meeting of the WCCC leaders would be in Canterbury in August, 1969. A decision should be made at that time.

What should they determine? Should they respond quickly in the affirmative, trusting the good will of the Kimbanguists? Should they seek a *pro forma* investigation, requisite for membership on the part of European-oriented churches from the Third World? Should they seek a full-scale investigation of the Kimbanguists, because this would be the first "nationally" focused communion from the Third World to seek admission which had not been sponsored by the parent denomination? Or should they just refuse the application, listening to the persons who claimed that the Kimbanguists now sought to "soak" the World Council of Churches for resources and money? An ecumenical wing of the WCC already existed in the Republic of Zaire

---

This case study was prepared by Professor Louis Weeks of the Louisville Presbyterian Theological Seminary as a basis for class discussion rather than to illustrate either effective or ineffective handling of a situation.

(formerly the Congo)—the CPC, the Congo Protestant Council. How should this council, of Methodist, Presbyterian, Disciples of Christ, Baptist, and other African communions descended from the missions of each denomination, be brought into the process? They had not endorsed the application, but whether active antipathy character-ized their relationships would be hard to ascertain. Members of the Central Committee reviewed the background and characteristics of the Kimbanguists.

Background: Belgian Control of the Congo

The Congo River Basin area, over 900,000 square miles of land with a diverse population of mostly Bantu tribespeople, was claimed by King Leopold II of Belgium as a private possession in 1885. Concessions were granted by the king to several international cartels for exploiting Congolese resources. The colony was transferred to the Belgian government, after allegations of immense cruelty on the part of the king's officers were validated and exposed in the Western press. Thus from 1908 until independence on June 30, 1960, it re-mained in Belgian hands.

The differing tribes of the Congo, with a host of languages and varied histories, were intentionally played off against one another by colonial authorities. Natural enmity may also have caused some of the strain which continues to the present day, however; and an-thropologists have identified at least seven "cultural clusters"—the Kongo, Mongo, Kuba, Lunda, Luba, Warena, and the Mangbetu-Azande. In short, the life of Congolese peoples under Belgian control was seldom easy, and almost always controlled in some fashion.

The Congo during the early and middle twentieth century repre-sented a major mission endeavor on the part of both Catholic and Protestant churches. Statistics of any kind are difficult to glean for the area, but by one account, in 1955 there were 490 Catholic "posts" and 244 Protestant. Almost 5,000 Catholic missionaries, with 1200 African assistants, served a Roman Catholic population of 3,455,084. The Protestant population of 704,254 was served by 1300 missionar-ies and about 900 African assistants. Thus over four million of the less than twelve and a half million inhabitants of the country in 1955 were either Catholic or Protestant, in recognized communions. For-eign missionaries controlled the various missions without exception.

Members of the Kimbanguist Church did not figure in the Chris-tian statistics of 1955, though, for that communion was banned by the Belgian government until just before the time of independence. The last deportations of Kimbanguist believers took place in 1957, two years after the survey quoted above and six years after the death of their founder, Simon Kimbangu, in an Elizabethtown prison.

Background: Simon Kimbangu

The founder of the church was born probably in 1889. His mother died when Simon was very young, and he lived most of his childhood with an aunt, Kinzembo. Thomas Comber and other missionaries educated Simon, and they baptized him also as a Baptist. He grew up to marry Mwilu Marie, and began farming in Nkamba, Thysville District, in the Lower Congo region. In addition to his other duties, Kimbangu practiced masonry and rudimentary mechanics. From time to time he would leave the village for a sojourn in Kinshasa (then Léopoldville), but he always returned home. Later he reminisced and interpreted these interludes as his selfish attempts to resist God's call and divine revelation.

But in March 1921, he acceded to Christ's call to preach and heal as a catechist for the Baptist Missionary Society (BMS). Certain of his mission because of a personal religious experience, he undertook to heal a woman in the nearby village of Kintondo. According to a Kimbanguist source, Kimbangu heard God say, "Take your pipe and your hat in your hand," and God led him into the woman's hut. The Catechist then said, "You are blessed in the name of Jesus Christ. Be healed." After leaving her, he talked with the woman's husband, who in turn found his wife well.

By April, people were flocking from all over the Lower Congo region, even coming from Kinshasa, to listen to the *ngunza* ("prophet") and perchance to receive healing for themselves and people they loved. The prophet preached that Jesus demanded an end to fetish worship, and the destroying of idols which prevent true worship of God. He also sought an end to tribal dancing, polygamy, and other acts he considered contrary to the gospel. The popularity of his preaching and his continued miracles brought thousands of Congolese on the pilgrimage to Nkamba. Workshops, mission schools, and industries were virtually deserted as the people left without warning. The white settlers and Belgian government officials, losing their personal and corporate servants, feared that Kimbangu was urging a general uprising and xenophobia. They feared he also encouraged a movement for national independence, nonpayment of taxes, and incited tribalism. Evidently at no time during his active ministry did Kimbangu seek to establish a new cult, sect, or denomination. Rather he continually employed Protestant texts and translations, and urged converts to support the work of the BMS. He also preached Biblical admonitions about the separation of Caesar's things from God's things, the messages of Old and New Testament generosity, and a type of Christian nonviolence.

Because of his growing reputation and news of his healings, Congolese Christian leaders came from various villages to work with Kimbangu. Church records indicate that on May 2 the prophet rejoiced in the work of one colleague, Ntwalani Thomas. He likewise received the services of seven other fellow prophets a few days later. Some, however, he "unmasked" as false prophets and healed them by casting out their demons. Immense agitation among the tribespeople resulted also in a "white backlash."

Because they believed the rumors that they themselves had generated, Belgian authorities sought to arrest Kimbangu throughout the summer of 1921, and they finally incarcerated him on September 12. He was found guilty of treason and a military court sentenced Kimbangu to die. King Albert I, successor to Leopold, "graciously" commuted the sentence to life imprisonment. Thus until his death Kimbangu remained in jail. He was subjected to continual humiliation by wardens and continuous exile in provinces of the Congo remote from his home.

Colonial oppression of the movement did not cease with acts against the founder himself. Those who confessed belief in Simon Kimbangu's *ngunzism,* which Belgian colonial authorities equated with "messianism," were deported throughout the various territories. Many of the Kimbanguists rallied around the new mission of the Salvation Army in the Congo, as a cover for their continuance in the movement. Most mission hospitals and schools refused to accept patients and students who were even alleged to be Kimbanguists. Another problem for the Kimbanguists was the appearance of various prophets claiming allegiance to Kimbangu though speaking of their new revelations from God. These persons tempted many of the followers of Kimbangu to desert the teachings of their former leader. Simon Mpadi, heading one such "schism," urged revitalization of tribal polygamy.

In response to these threats to the movement and other acts of oppression, the church organized as quickly as possible when independence had been promised. Joseph Diangienda, the youngest of Kimbangu's three children, was proclaimed the hierarchical head of the new denomination. He early in his administration refused a tendered offer from national political leaders to make the denomination a "state church" of the country. But flourish it did so that its numbers exceeded a million in the Congo alone, with other outposts growing in neighboring countries and especially in Angola (which remained a Portuguese colony).

Kimbanguist Theology

A summary of the chief tenets of Kimbanguist theology had been made by the World Council of Churches in a study published the year before. In this 1967 document which M. B. Handspicker and Lukas Vischer composed on four nonparticipating Christian bodies (in the WCC), the following assessment had been voiced:

Doctrine

Simon Kimbangu was not a theologian. He did not leave any confessional writings, nor any well-defined doctrinal teaching. According to all the reliable witnesses, his preaching was simply "orthodox," in accordance with the preaching of the Baptist pastors and catechists whom he had known. In a sense, there is no special Kimbanguist theology.

The Church of Jesus Christ on earth through Simon Kimbangu is a Christian Church which regards Jesus Christ as the Saviour of the world. It is firmly biblical. During his short ministry, Simon Kimbangu always had a Bible in his hand, and the Kimbanguist pastors still do so. The worship centers around reading the Bible and explaining it. The hymns, which are of a revivalist kind, are clearly Christocentric, and direct the piety of the faithful towards the redeeming sacrifice on the Cross.

It is a universalist Church, in the sense that it believes itself called "to bear the message of Our Lord Jesus Christ to all the countries in the world, as enjoined by Holy Scripture" (*Statement of Principles*, p. 4). It addresses itself to all tribes, all races, all nations. It is neither racialistic nor anti-foreign, although it is firmly African in its organization and leadership. It recognizes the validity of the other Christian Churches and has never tried to break away from Christian tradition on any point. On the contrary, it is very anxious to become a humble member of the ecumenical movement.

Like the Gospel itself, this Church considers the body to be just as important as the soul; no clear distinction is drawn between the spiritual and the secular, between spiritual life and social life. The healing of the sick therefore plays an important role, as it does in the Gospels, but prayer, the laying on of hands, and immersion in the miraculous spring at Nkamba, are practiced in all simplicity, in a healthy atmosphere, silently and prosaically. For "the healing obtained by a sick person who appeals to the intervention of the Holy Spirit is due only to his own faith" (*Statement of Principles,* p. 4).

The Church feels deeply responsible for the nation, for the civic society in which it exists, and struggles hard for social progress through justice and peace. However, it takes care not to interfere with the responsibilities of the secular authorities. It recommends loyalty to the state.

In its tradition the Church is Puritan; this is in accordance with the preaching of the prophet (Kimbangu) who stressed the importance of practical conduct rather than of dogma. Consequently the Church is categorically opposed to all practice of sorcery and fetishism; it insists on pure morals (strict monogamy, decent clothing, etc.), prohibits dancing (which is suspected of always being more or less pagan or erotic), and also prohibits smoking, eating pork, or drinking alcohol. Sanctions are imposed on those who break these rules, even so far as exclusion from the Church. Although not strictly pacifist, the Church condemns all recourse to violence, even on the part of the State, and from the very beginning it has practiced non-violent resistance to evil.

The Decision

Now the Central Committee must make its decision. Was the communion sufficiently "Christian" to warrant admission? What about the fact that grass-roots suspicion of the Kimbanguists might alienate the constituent denominations of the CPC? Should there be strictures on the amount of funds Kimbanguists could receive from the body? Most importantly, were their beliefs identifiable regarding Jesus Christ and the nature of the gospel?

BIBLIOGRA HY

The following materials were used in the preparation of this case and are recommended for further study.

Andersson, Efriam. *Churches at the Grassroots.* London: Lutterworth Press, 1968.

Barrett, David B. *Schism and Renewal in Africa.* Nairobi: Oxford University Press, 1968.

Handspicker, M. B., and Vischer, Lukas. *An Ecumenical Exercise.* Geneva: World Council of Churches, 1967.

Oosthuizen, G. C. *Post-Christianity in Africa.* Wm. B. Eerdmans Publishing Company, 1968.

15

Rosemary Radford Ruether
(A.D. 1974)

Rosemary Radford Ruether was looking forward to grappling with serious and central issues. She was scheduled to address a consultation of twenty feminist theologians at a leading American university. It comprised most of the women holding professorial posts in seminaries plus a majority of women working on Ph.D.'s in religion. Just days before, on September 9, 1974, *Time* magazine had appeared hailing her as one of eleven "religious superstars." She found the publication of such a list including one Black, one Latin, one Native American, and herself as the token woman both laughable and tragic. She felt that it obscured the primary purpose of liberation theology —to de-privatize theology and to recognize the social structures of the conflict. Now she could forget her designation as a "shaper and shaker of the Christian faith" and speak to "Sexism and God-Talk" with these women with whom she felt solidarity. How may women respond to a Father-God whose transcendence has been used to justify social structures of male domination? In what sense does the maleness of Jesus constitute an impediment to his being seen as a redeemer of or for women? What role can women have in a church structured around a male, clerical caste? How can women be saved from oppression and self-alienation and enter into a new creation? How should she open these issues in depth for these women who like herself were deeply immersed in them by experience and scholarly study?

This case study was prepared by Professor Jack Rogers of Fuller Theological Seminary and student Joan Cathey. It is intended as a basis for class discussion rather than to illustrate either effective or ineffective handling of a situation.

Background

Rosemary Radford was born in St. Paul, Minnesota, a descendant of English families who came to this country in the Revolutionary War era. Her father was an Anglican of the twice-a-year variety, and her mother was a devout Catholic "of independent mind." Young Rosemary grew up with little feeling of the restraint or authoritarianism of the church. There was great respect for classical education in the family, but she became the first professional scholar. Rosemary attended Catholic girls seminaries in Washington, D.C., and Greece until her father's death when she was twelve. Several years later the family moved to her mother's native state of California and Rosemary attended a public high school in La Jolla.

During her first year of college, Rosemary Radford's "rather elitist, but fairly secure Catholicism" collapsed under historical study. She concluded at this time that either God was unjust, or heaven and hell did not exist. "If there is meaning in ongoing human life, it must be sought somehow in solidarity with the race, with the earth, with the matrix that binds us all together, not in the isolated self." The decision was made to believe nothing because "the church" taught it, but only because it was personally believable.

Rosemary Radford's interest in art led her to Scripps College, Claremont, California, with the intention of studying fine arts and humanities. Through the influence of a charismatic teacher, Robert Palmer, her interests shifted dramatically to classics and ancient history. "It was Palmer, the believing pagan, who first taught me to think theologically. . . . Through him I discovered the meaning of religious symbols, not as extrinsic doctrines, but as living metaphors of human existence." This was the beginning of being interested in religious ideas in a new way.

From there, Rosemary Radford turned to the study of the Bible, Christian origins, and theology. After reaching the conclusion that Catholic scholarship lacked historical consciousness, and Protestant scholarship was limited by "fundamental Biblical intolerance," she developed a tendency toward dialectical thinking. She was suspicious of any idea that was one side of a dualism. At this time, she came to find that nuns, priests, and theologians were not authorities but "people with problems." Now she no longer had a guilt complex whose resolution had only two options—capitulate or leave the church—but she began to feel responsible for the church, rather than it being responsible for her. A year before college graduation Rosemary Radford married Herman Ruether, a scholar who enjoyed the library stacks as much as she did. Three children born while both were in graduate school working on Ph.D.'s did not change the pattern of a day devoted primarily to study.

About this time, Rosemary Radford Ruether felt that her interest in religion could not be satisfied by a "head trip," but needed to be nourished by an experience of worship and prayer in community. She became a frequent visitor to Saint Andrew's Priory in Valyermo. In the late '50s, St. Andrew's represented the best in theology and liturgical renewal that had been developing in Europe. It also became a center for a group of people which the press dubbed an "underground church," demanding that the church do something about civil rights and peace issues. For four years the Valyermo community was Rosemary Ruether's "spiritual home." It was there also that she wrote much of her Ph.D. dissertation on Gregory Nazianzen, a fourth-century Greek church father. Her experience there is "fixed in memory in a golden moment where time intersects with eternity." Two problems disrupted the continuance of that "golden moment." The St. Andrew's community was blamed for some of the ferment of the early '60s by James Cardinal McIntyre, the conservative Roman Catholic archbishop of Los Angeles. Vincent Martin, Ruether's spiritual "guru," was pressured out of the monastery and the core of the protest movement was broken. Perhaps worse for her was the realization that the liberalism of the priests at St. Andrew's was, as she said, "bounded by limits of authority and tradition that could not account for many things that I knew." This rigid concept of authority made thinking impossible and made a decision against the Catholic Church inevitable.

At this point, Ruether made a move to leave the church, then discovered that although she could not be reconverted to the traditional concept of authority, she could not leave the church either. At this time, she said, "I am personally convinced that believing that you are infallible is the surest way to become accident prone." Later she was to state, "It is the infallibility complex, which Popes and Revolutionary dictators both share, which needs to be exposed as idolatry and demonic possession." However, of her decision to remain in the church, she said, "The Church, like myself, was an unfinished possibility. Therein lies hope for us both."

Until age twenty-five, Rosemary Ruether's life was severely academic. Then during the late '60s, she became a political activist. Ruether declared: "This was partly through my husband, whose field of political science made it more necessary for him to read the newspapers than I had been accustomed to do, and partly through the press of events of the sixties that began to catch up the university and religious worlds that I occupied." In the summer of 1966 she worked with the Delta ministry in Mississippi and later in Watts after the riots there. Looking back on this period, she declared: "One began to connect the historic structures of oppression: race, class, sex, colonialism, finally the destructive patterns of human society toward nature, in an integrated vision of social contradictions and demands for social revolution." In her own life and thought she traveled from working in civil rights, to peace activism, and on to revolutionary analysis.

While rejecting the demand for "relevance" which "insists on knowing only what the individual self had directly experienced," Ruether discovered that it was impossible for her to return to the kind of "pure scholarship" for which she had been trained. In 1967 both she and her husband accepted teaching positions in Washington, D.C. Rosemary Ruether's post was in the School of Religion at Howard University, a predominantly Black institution. By choice the Ruethers located in the Black community and raised their children in Black schools. Rosemary Ruether stated: "I was determined to live and teach in the Black community, so I would not forget what I had seen."

In 1972–73, she taught at Harvard Divinity School. "In my experience with seminary education," she commented on this experience, "there seems to be a growing division into two hostile and non-communicating camps: the classical scholars and the action-reflection people." She felt the wrath of both groups as she tried to bridge between the two. "To build a human way of operating, even in the framework of a classroom, finally demands a revolution in our value system, our personality structures and our socio-economic organization."

Ruether now found herself variously described as a "Catholic theologian (with the exact status of 'Catholic' uncertain), a feminist, and a social activist." She did not, she said, set out to become any of these things. They simply happened along the way by an inevitable logic.

Sexism and God-Talk

The time had come for Rosemary Radford Ruether to deliver her paper. She began: "It is not enough to declare that God is Spirit and therefore 'He' is not literally male, and then assume that all can go on as before. More is involved than the pronoun 'He.' The very imagination by which God is envisioned in a certain relation to creation is in question. One can no longer assume either the finality of that revelation or the basis of its tradition. [Revelation's] images of God, creation, redemption, and future hope are interwoven with themes oppressive to half of the human race." "One has to ask whether much that we have taken to be 'of God' were not in fact sanctifying sexual, not to mention class and racial, domination by a particular leadership group."

Feminism demands an expansion of the sources of symbols for theology. They must include hidden and forbidden traditions, for example, heresies such as "feminine folk religion, charismatic sects, beguines, the persecution of witches [in order] to find out what alternatives were being rejected."

The relationship of God to creation is separate and transcendent. "The world is to be seen as something outside of and other than God, which He makes from nothing, which exists as an inferior and dependent reality. Only this language preserves the majesty and otherness of God."

This is the language of male experience, i.e., toolmaker to object made. "The absolute split between God as transcendent mind and the world as dependent object seems to me to be modeled after the self-concept of leadership males. [This] provides the mandate for the patriarchal class to relate to women, servants, slaves and property in the same way as the Deity relates to the world. She [the woman] is seen as part of nature, while he, like God, is sovereign of nature." "This seems to be a male model of transcendence (God being prior to and exalted above the universe and being apart from it) which historically created a vicious misogynism in Christianity."

Ruether declared her rejection of the Western view of God as a "neurotic, authoritarian parent, who can never let 'His' children become self-actualizing adults. . . . In order to affirm the absoluteness of God as the source of power, one has to deny the freedom of the creaturely will to do anything of itself other than sin." She stated her preference for the concept of God as the divine Matrix (a place or enveloping element within which something originates, takes form, or develops) so that God may be seen as "an empowering spirit who founds our freedom for self-actualization."

The Redemptive Power of Jesus

Rosemary Ruether shared her feeling that feminism may "not be able to accept the finality for the basis for redemption available in Christianity." She said that "the identification of women with the material side of the body-spirit split created a model of redemption which was misogynist. Women could be redeemed by Jesus only by an alienation, not only from their bodily, but from their female natures, whereas males were seen as restored by Jesus to that spirituality which is intrinsically male."

"What is unrevealed," Ruether asserted, "is not the female half of a male world, but the whole humanity of both men and women beyond sexism. Jesus as a particular person may have been on the way to this. But Jesus as a male symbol cannot mediate this reality in a sexist world."

"Women must reject the idea that Jesus is the final word, even in order to affirm Jesus as one revelatory word in the midst of an incompleted redemption.... Women have a problem with Christology as the elevation of Jesus to the status of God's last word in history. Jesus is theologically credible, not as the final word, but as that crucified hope who locates us where we are in history, forsaken by the Father-God and looking forward to that new humanity which has not yet been revealed."

She continued by saying that "Jesus is a smashed beginning, broken by the power of domination, awaiting that future revelation which still eludes us all.... From that realm of unfulfilled possibility he does not reign as Lord in order to sanction the earthly rule of a Church which re-establishes the male ruling class domination 'in His name.'"

The Integration of Women Into the Church

According to this feminist view, the church is the strongly entrenched foe of women. One reason for this, Ruether contended, is that "Christian culture took over and absorbed the classical view of man and its myth of salvation, and so molded its social institutions accordingly that it now finds itself the foe of the new culture bearers of its own original tradition. This is nowhere more true than in the social structure and culture of that group which is most closely associated with the Church—the clergy. They appear as almost the last bastion of the 'old humanity' where anti-feminine, anti-bodily patriarchalism still reigns. This means that the Church can only recover its own original gospel of the new creation of the resurrected by dying to a culture and social structure with which it has most deeply identified itself. This also means that the avant garde of the 'new humanity' have lost their own roots in finding it all but impossible to recognize the Christian Church as anything but the oldest and most entrenched of their foes."

The church cannot relate to women, she said, because "the historical Church still represents the caste-oriented, state-of-life mode of leadership. In both its exclusive maleness and its clericalness, it exhibits what has now become an archaic form of social relationships."

"It will be impossible to integrate women into the present celibate, clerical structure of the priesthood because that structure was set up to express the dominating, female-rejecting *logos* and cannot survive in its present state except through the maintenance of that presupposition."

It has been claimed that the masculinity of Catholicism is balanced by the feminine principle in Mariology. Not so, said Ruether. Rather, this patriarchal feminine principle defined a passive, receptive self in relation to male activity and domination. For example:

Father-God in relation to feminine creation

A male Christ as bridegroom to the female church as bride

A male husband to a female wife

"Mariology inculcates that spirit of perfect submission to the commands of hierarchal authority. [Thus] all [male-female] relations become either sadistic or masochistic."

The Protestant Church does not escape blame in this area, since it has the same theological root of the feminine in its feminine image of the church in relation to God the Father, and the relation of wife to husband. The Protestant symbol for this submissive feminine principle is represented ideally by the pastor's wife.

A Possible Solution

Rosemary Ruether outlined her solution to the problem of sexism in theological language and action. It is found in what she called the "double conversion process."

Women are impelled to move toward masculinity for liberation from dependency. This creates a double bind for them. They suffer from both self-alienation and self-hatred. Ruether said, "It is the masculine definition of the relation of the self to others and the world which is the root of sexism." The double conversion process "must seek a breakthrough which dissolves both sides of the false dualism, psychically and socially. Feminine can be good only when [it] no longer exists in a dependency relation to people in power, but proceeds from an empowered self."

"Males," she said, "can be unoppressive in their search for their own repressed, emotive, receptive, somatic self only in doing so by supporting wholeness and independence for women."

"Feminism can aim at nothing less than a new creation. Not only must women be empowered to think and act and men be put in touch with their receptive and nurturing powers, but the processes by which these qualities have been related to each other in the self and social personality must be so totally transformed that one can no longer speak of them as activity and passivity, much less as masculinity and feminity, but as the dialectic of mutual reciprocity by which people actualize themselves at the same time that they support the actualization of others. This does not mean the 'reduction of the world to a sameness,' but the flowering of individuality in community released from the reductionism of sexist stereotypes."

"Theologically this vision can be called redemption. This means the reconciliation of humanity with itself; the reconciliation of people to each other and of humanity to nature. The reconciliation of creation with itself is the concrete manifestation of the reconciliation of humanity with God. But creation can be reconciled with God only if God 'Himself' is converted from his patriarchalism to become the ground of reciprocity in creation. The 'death of God the Father' is the overthrowing of that alienated image of male egoism which sanctifies all the relations of domination and subjugation in the world, in order that the community of life can be born. This is that new creation glimpsed but unrealized in the gospel, which declared that, in Christ, 'the dividing wall of hostility has been broken down in order to reconcile those who have been alienated from one another' (Eph. 2:14)."

The Probing of Peers

The address was concluded. Now Rosemary Ruether eagerly awaited the response of her feminist colleagues.

QUES: How does the double conversion take place? Via the church? Political process?

R.R.: The church is very peripheral to social change, but religion has been a chief sanctifier of oppressive social structures. . . . [We] need some sensitized people and a multiplicity of structures to play off against each other. I couldn't survive as a theologian if the churches got together. We need and can use anarchy—by skipping from place to place to hide.

QUES: What about words? Can we get new ones?

R.R.: One needs a generic word. We need to include "she/he" and not eliminate "man." As long as you have sexist social structures it will play back in the language.

QUES: Why do you avoid the third Person of the Trinity?

R.R.: I could identify what I've been trying to say about God with the Holy Spirit. Hymns that are relatively nonsexist are those to the Spirit. I don't talk about the Holy Spirit because it reminds us of the spirit-body split. I find in the early fathers

a tremendous struggle to overcome these dualisms. It is a
battle they eventually lose. But they try. What I'm saying is
what the early fathers were struggling to express.

QUES: To say that Jesus was "smashed" is to deny the resurrection.

R.R.: I only want to deny a resurrection that reestablishes the oppressive domination.

QUES: The resurrection is a denial of the incarnation. Putting Jesus
at the right hand of God is starting all over—on the wrong
road.

R.R.: Incarnation is the people's response to Jesus as the embodiment of God. Jesus didn't teach it!

QUES: People's identity with Jesus is an affirmation of their own
divinity.

R.R.: In the New Testament, Jesus is a paradigm for all people.

QUES: All my friends in the women's movement are now divorced.
That's not an option (economically, socially, etc.) for most
women. We have to have other options. Men have to grow
up and take on their own liberation—and not depend on
women to do it for them.

R.R.: I just came from a large denomination's pastors conference.
I was the first woman ever to address the conference. They
wanted Gloria Steinem but decided she was too pretty. It
ended up that the white women clergy and the black pastors
got together. The white pastors (90 percent) were so sad and
afraid. I wanted to say, "I've not come to castrate you, but to
give you new virility."

QUES: The men are self-castrated—though they project it on the
women. Other men try to keep them in their place. Clergy
have been housewives to their congregations and then dominated women. Now when women get uppity, men don't have
anything to hold on to.

R.R.: [We] must indicate to men their stake in liberation—that the
real powers that castrate them are not women, but the Penta-
gon.

R.R.: Both in church tradition and in everyday conversation the
highest praise for women by men is as the better half of
themselves. It must finally dawn on a man that this woman
over there is not another half of himself—but an independent
person.

As the discussion concluded, Rosemary Radford Ruether reflected
on the situation. Rethinking foundational concepts of God, Christology, the church, and the human self was difficult but necessary.

Had she opened fresh and fruitful perspectives for the thinking of these feminist theologians?

BIBLIOGRAPHY

Some of the material in this case study was taken from prepublication forms of manuscripts which Ms. Ruether provided. The following sources along with personal interviews and letters are gratefully acknowledged.

Ruether, Rosemary Radford. "The Becoming of Women in Church and Society," *Cross Currents,* Vol. XVII, Fall 1967, pp. 418–426.

_____. "Beginnings: An Intellectual Autobiography," in *Journeys— The Impact of Personal Experience on Religious Thought.* Edited by Gregory Baum. Paulist/Newman Press, 1975.

_____. "The Cult of Womanhood," *Commonweal,* Vol. XLIX, Nov. 9, 1973, pp. 127–132.

_____. "Male Chauvinist Theology and the Anger of Women," *Cross Currents,* Vol. XXI, Spring 1971, pp. 173–185.

_____. "Outlines for a Theology of Liberation," *Dialog,* Vol. XI, Autumn 1972, pp. 252–257.

_____. "Sexism and God-Talk." Unpublished address, 1974, pp. 1–20.

_____. "Sexism and the Theology of Liberation," *The Christian Century,* Vol. XC, Dec. 12, 1972, pp. 1224–1229.

_____. "Women's Liberation in Historical and Theological Perspective," *Soundings,* Vol. LIII, Winter 1970, pp. 363–373.

For Further Study
Ruether, Rosemary Radford. *Liberation Theology.* Paulist/Newman Press 1972.

_____. *New Woman/New Earth: Sexist Ideologies and Human Liberation.* The Seabury Press, Inc., 1975.

Ruether, Rosemary Radford, ed. *Religion and Sexism.* Simon & Schuster, Inc., 1974.

16
The International Congress
on World Evangelization (A.D. 1974)

Billy Graham sat forward in his seat and anxiously awaited the words of the speaker on his headphones. The interpreter's voice resonated with the message of South American René Padilla:

> I enjoyed the advantage of not having my earphones on so I didn't have to hear what he [the moderator, Rev. Maurice Ray, from Switzerland] was saying about me.

Graham was relieved that the initial words were spoken in a light-hearted manner. He suspected that the ensuing message would be highly controversial—as had been so many others at the Congress— inciting some to fervent applause, others to a reserved, perhaps even zealous, disagreement.

Billy Graham listened to this message with a particular consternation that no one else in that meeting shared, for this meeting of the International Congress on World Evangelization was his own brain-child. He had conceived of this Congress shortly after the gathering of several hundred Evangelical leaders in West Berlin in 1966. After that World Congress on Evangelism, Graham began to assess the feasibility of a larger, more diverse assembly of Evangelical Christians. The Berlin Congress of 1966 had largely failed to deal with the pressing social and political problems of that turbulent decade. The 1966 meeting as well did not touch upon some very important issues of church-growth strategy. In addition there were still undercurrents of doctrinal differences among Evangelicals. This next Congress would thus have a particularly heavy emphasis upon evangelical

This case study was prepared by Professor Jack Rogers of Fuller Theological Seminary in cooperation with students Michael Gallion, Gloryanna Hees, and Daniel Price. It is intended as a basis for class discussion rather than to illustrate either effective or ineffective handling of a situation.

social concern and strategy for spreading the gospel message to every ethnic group upon the face of the earth. Would the Congress point significant directions in these areas? Would Evangelicals unite, or would there be doctrinal divisions? Billy Graham wondered as he listened.

Calling the International Congress on World Evangelization

For ten days nearly four thousand people from 150 countries met at the Palais de Beaulieu in Lausanne, Switzerland, to discuss Biblical foundations and strategies for spreading the gospel of Jesus Christ throughout the world. "Let the Earth Hear His Voice" was the theme of the Congress held July 16–25, 1974. The attendants at the Congress were there primarily because of the efforts of Billy Graham and his close associates. Graham's title at this Congress was Honorary Chairman. He, along with Executive Chairman Jack Dain, from Australia, had appointed a Convening Committee of some thirty persons, comprised of many who had been involved at some time or another with the Billy Graham Evangelistic Association (BGEA). This committee was chosen by Graham and many of his friends (among them Bill Bright, Leighton Ford, Stan Mooneyhan, Harold Lindsell, and Don Hoke). After placing themselves on the committee, they included persons from five other continents. Many of the 3,800 registrants were chosen by the committee directly. But, in an attempt to avoid provincialism, the committee solicited names for potential registrants (whom they did not know) from individuals whom they did know and trust. They made serious efforts to send invitations to people who could represent the Third World. The delegates came as individuals, not as representatives of either churches or mission agencies. Many of those who were asked to attend were offered scholarships.

The Convening Committee also selected the speakers for the Congress. Each person who agreed to address the plenary session on some specific topic was asked to draw up a paper. The paper was then distributed to all the registrants several months prior to the Congress. The variety of speakers clearly posed the issues of social involvement, missions strategy, and doctrinal diversity implicit in the composition of the Congress.

Social Concerns

René Padilla, a native Ecuadorian, was asked by the committee to be one of the plenary session speakers. Padilla had attended Wheaton College, receiving both a B.A. in Philosophy and an M.A. in Dogmatic Theology. While there he married an American girl. He then traveled to England, where he obtained a Ph.D. in New Testament Studies at the University of Manchester. Padilla was affiliated with the Plymouth Brethren denomination.

At the time when Padilla was asked to speak, he held the position of Latin-American Secretary-General of the International Fellowship of Evangelical Students in Buenos Aires—a South American sister organization of Inter-Varsity Christian Fellowship. He had been editor as well of *Certeza* magazine, coauthored a book, *Quién Es Cristo Hoy?*, and written theological articles in both North and South American journals and periodicals.

Padilla's most noteworthy theological stances included: (1) a heavy emphasis upon the necessity of Christian social involvement; (2) the dire need of a truly Latin-American theology for the Latin-American Protestants; (3) the rejection of the Marxist-oriented "Liberation Theology" as the answer to Latin America's needs; and (4) vehement criticism of North American "culture Christianity."

René Padilla's Speech

After expressions of gratitude to those who had responded to his paper, Padilla delivered his plenary session message. He emphasized the four elements of his stance as presented in his pre-Congress study paper, entitled "Evangelism and the World." He asserted:

When the church lets itself be squeezed into the mold of the world, it loses the capacity to see and, even more, to denounce, the social evils in its own situation. Like the color-blind person who is able to distinguish certain colors, but not others, the worldly church recognizes the personal vices traditionally condemned within its ranks, but is unable to see the evil features of its surrounding culture. In my understanding, this is the only way one can explain, for example, how it is possible for American culture Christianity to integrate racial and class segregation into its strategy for world evangelization. How can a church that, for the sake of numerical expansion, deliberately opts for segregation speak to a divided world?

At this juncture Billy Graham experienced a slightly nervous twinge welling up from the depths of his stomach, for René Padilla was proceeding with a polemic against certain factions at the Congress who had discussed strategy for world evangelization. Just the previous day, Dr. Donald A. McGavran, dean emeritus of Fuller Theological Seminary's School of World Mission, had spoken on "The Dimensions of World Evangelization." In his presentation before the plenary session he reiterated ten dimensions of world evangelization. He began:

> I stressed, *first,* that Christ commands world evangelization, salvation comes only through faith in Jesus Christ, the only inspired Scripture is the Bible, and while horizontal reconciliation of man with man is good, it is no substitute for vertical reconciliation of man with God. *Second,* comes the biblical fact that God accepts all cultures as equally valid vehicles for the Gospel.

As Graham reflected on McGavran's address and Padilla's speech he began to suspect that there might be increasing disagreement because of each speaker's markedly different emphasis.

As Graham listened, Padilla concluded:

> Our greatest need is a more biblical Gospel and a more faithful church. We may go away from this Congress with a nice set of papers and statements that will be filed away and forgotten, and with the memories of a big, impressive world meeting. Or we may go away with the conviction that we have magic formulas for the conversion of people. My own hope and prayer is that we go away with a repentant attitude with regard to our enslavement to the world and our arrogant triumphalism, with a sense of helplessness to break away from our bonds, and yet also with a great confidence in God, the Father of our Lord Jesus Christ, who "by the power at work within us is able to do far more abundantly than all that we ask or think, to him be glory in the church and in Christ Jesus to all generations, for ever and ever. Amen."

Billy Graham left the morning meeting with somewhat ambivalent feelings toward Padilla's message. The audience's applause for Padilla had been sporadic—but vehement. Yet, many of the attendants at the Congress perhaps failed to perceive the social dynamics that went on both within and without the Palais de Beaulieu.

Missions Strategy

The committee engaged in the preparatory work of selecting speakers, headed by Paul Little of Inter-Varsity Christian Fellowship, faced a dilemma in choosing a speaker to present the topic of cross-cultural evangelism. Possibly the most qualified man for the job was Dr. Ralph Winter, professor of the Historical Development of the Christian Movement in the School of World Mission at Fuller Theological Seminary. Little was reluctant about naming a second member of this school's faculty to speak since Dr. Donald McGavran had already been invited.

Winter, for his part, had reservations about whether Lausanne would go beyond the emphasis in most evangelism congresses for local efforts at evangelism. He wanted an Edinburgh II, an idea proposed in June 1972 by the Baptist Dr. Luther Copeland, president of the (U.S.) Association of Professors of Missions, at their annual meeting. Winter noted that Edinburgh (1910) was different from Lausanne because "it was strictly a delegated body, made up of official representatives of missionary societies, and it was a deliberative body, seeking to formulate policy for the years ahead. While it possessed no legislative authority, it could suggest, and because it was composed of leaders of the various societies there was reason to suppose that its recommendations would be followed by action."

Ralph Winter was tendered and accepted an invitation to address the International Congress on World Evangelization. He hoped to throw additional light on the dimensions of the task remaining in· world evangelization. On Saturday, July 20, he rose to address the Congress on the subject "The Highest Priority: Cross-Cultural Evangelism." Of the fourteen plenary speakers, he was one of only four who had been involved in a cross-cultural mission. Prior to his present position he had served for fifteen years under the Commission on Ecumenical Mission and Relations of The United Presbyterian Church U.S.A. For ten of those years, he was a missionary to Guatemala assigned to leadership development among Mayan Indians. His preparation for service included an engineering degree from California Institute of Technology, a theology degree from Princeton Theological Seminary, and a Ph.D. from Cornell University in the field of Descriptive Linguistics and Cultural Anthropology.

Ralph Winter's Address

When the time came for Ralph Winter to address the Congress, he hoped to establish the number one priority as the church's mission to "Let the Earth Hear His Voice," summed up by his closing statement, "We must have radically new efforts of cross-cultural evangelism in order to effectively witness to two billion three hundred eighty-seven million people, and we cannot believe that we can continue to virtually ignore this highest priority." By "virtually ignore," Winter referred to the widespread—and, he felt, false—assumption that getting Christians to reach out in their own language and culture wherever they are in the world was a strategy that could reach most of the non-Christians. To disprove this, he presented careful estimates of the actual numbers of non-Christians within evangelizing range of existing churches around the world. By these figures he then showed that 87 percent of the non-Christians of the world are sufficiently distant culturally so as to require the setting up of new congregations for their kind.

To get at this problem, he presented a method of distinguishing different types of evangelism by degrees of cultural distance—a scale unrelated to geographic distance. E-0 evangelism is directed to those affiliated with a church who have had no valid Christian experience. E-1 evangelism is carrying the gospel to people in one's own language and culture. E-2 evangelism requires going to people of a different but similar language and culture (namely, from the U.S.A. to rural Mexico), people just far enough away to need separate congregations in order best to reach their own people, whether in the same country or not. E-3 evangelism involves relating to people of radically different languages and cultures (namely, if an Anglo–North American tried to evangelize Navajos in Arizona or persons in the Far East who had had no exposure to Western culture). If more than 13 percent of the 2.7 billion who have not heard the gospel of Christ are to be reached, more than E-1 evangelism will be required. Trained specialists, not necessarily Westerners, able to adapt to other cultures and their customs must be employed in E-2 and E-3 evangelism.

"E-0, E-1, E-2, and E-3 are categories designed to help us talk about a cultural situation," Winter had said. "All have to do with the *degree* of cultural distance between the evangelists and those to be evangelized. . . . Local Christians who don't recognize that they cannot evangelize and bring into their local fellowship their culturally different or prejudice-separated near neighbors will not be effective evangelists. Thus, although there are millions of Christians in India, unless they understand that their near neighbors of different caste, culture, and/or language must be reached by E-2 or E-3 evangelists, they will not win them to Christ."

Doctrinal Divisions

As the Congress drew to a close a confessional statement was prepared which Billy Graham and others hoped the participants would sign. The Lausanne Covenant was meant to summarize what had occurred, demonstrate the unity of evangelicals and point directions for their future labors.

After many, many hours of toil and prayerful searching, John Stott, rector of All Souls' Church, London, presented in the Lausanne Covenant what he and the other members of the five-man team charged with preparing it thought those participating in the Congress were saying.

Francis Schaeffer, director of the L'Abri Fellowship, feeling that Evangelicals were abandoning Scripture, refused to sign the document on the grounds that the section on "The Authority and Power of the Bible" did not represent the Word of God as being inerrant.

Stott and his drafting committee rewrote that section so as to present a statement to the last session of the Congress which would gain favor with the supporters of Schaeffer and yet meet with the approval of the other attendees.

Francis Schaeffer had wended his way slowly down the Swiss Alps from his home in the village of Huemoz to attend the International Congress on World Evangelization at Lausanne. He had been invited to present a paper on "Form and Freedom in the Church," but he also had another purpose in mind: to battle for doctrinal purity. Against liberal theology, he planned to challenge the Evangelicals to practice the orthodoxy of Scripture.

The conflict between the conservatives and liberals within the Presbyterian Church during the 1930's left its mark on Schaeffer and conditioned his feelings that people in our present day were also abandoning the Word of God in Scripture. His great struggle evolved around maintaining:

. . . a Christianity which has balance, not only exegetically, and intellectually, but also in the area of reality and beauty; an insistence that beginning with the Christian system as God has given it to men in the verbalized propositional revelation of the Bible one can move along and find every area of life is touched by truth and song.

Beginning at Westminster Theological Seminary, Schaeffer left with a dissident group led by Carl McIntire and participated in the founding of Faith Theological Seminary where he was graduated in 1938. He served three pastorates during a period of about ten years. During this time he and his wife, Edith, began a ministry called Children for Christ. In 1947 they moved to Europe to work with children during post-World War II reconstruction. He also shared in the establishment in 1948 of the International Council of Christian Churches headed by McIntire. Schaeffer traveled extensively in Europe working with churches to help them understand the errors in modern-day theology. During an eighteen-month furlough in the United States in 1953–54, Schaeffer resigned from the various organizations which had been supporting him and decided to establish his own independent work. With his wife and family he settled down in Huemoz, Switzerland, where a ministry to young people began in 1955, with students and other people coming from all over the world to study under Schaeffer. As the number of students increased, buildings and chalets were added which came to form the L'Abri Fellowship—a community for study, communal living and labor.

Francis Schaeffer's Statement

Conflict over the nature of the Bible became apparent on Tuesday, July 23, 1974, when Schaeffer in his address to the Congress stated:

First, we must say if evangelicals are to be evangelicals, we must not compromise our view of Scripture.

We must say with sadness that in some places, seminaries, institutions, and individuals who are known as evangelical no longer hold to a full view of Scripture. The issue is clear: is the Bible true truth and infallible wherever it speaks, including where it touches history and the cosmos, or is it only in some sense revelational where it touches religious subjects?

Schaeffer continued:

The heart of neo-orthodox existential theology is that the Bible gives us a quarry out of which to hew religious experience but that the Bible contains mistakes where it touches that which is verifiable—namely history and science.

The issue is whether the Bible gives propositional truth (that is, truth that may be stated in propositions) where it touches history and the cosmos, and this all the way back to pre-Abrahamic history, all the way back to the first eleven chapters of Genesis, or whether instead of that it is only meaningful where it touches that which is considered religious.

Schaeffer felt that no statement on the Bible and its authority could be accepted as "safe" if the word "inerrant" was omitted. He went on to call for a separation of those evangelicals who held to "inerrancy" from those who did not: "Evangelicalism is not consistently evangelical unless there is a line drawn between those who take a full view of Scripture and those who do not."

Early in the Congress a rough draft of the Covenant was circulated which said,

> We affirm the divine inspiration, truthfulness, and authority of both Old and New Testament Scriptures in their entirety as the only written word of God and the only infallible rule of faith and practice.

Well over one thousand suggested changes were considered in preparing the final copy, including those from a group gathered around Francis Schaeffer and his stand on the "inerrancy" of the Bible. Expecting to gain the favor of the Schaefferites, the final version of the Covenant read,

> We affirm the divine inspiration, truthfulness, and authority of both Old and New Testament Scriptures in their entirety as the only written word of God, without error in all that it affirms, and the only infallible rule of faith and practice.

Another group, who called themselves the "radical Christians," including René Padilla, felt that even the revised document did not go far enough in dealing with societal problems. The day before the Congress ended, they presented their own covenant called "A Response to Lausanne."

Billy Graham, standing with John Stott on the platform at the close of the Congress, signed both documents—the Lausanne Covenant and the Response to Lausanne. As Graham penned his signature before the large gathering of evangelicals, he wondered if the radical Christians and the followers of Francis Schaeffer would sign the Lausanne Covenant.

Graham pondered the successes and failures of the Congress. Could four thousand "Evangelical" Christians from such varied backgrounds ever attain the working unity necessary to evangelize the world? Were the doctrinal, methodological, and social schisms so great that cooperation among these persons was impossible? The aura of the Lausanne Congress had been one of enthusiasm. The content of the messages oftentimes exposed factionalism and diversity. Which would win out? . . . Only time would tell.

BIBLIOGRAPHY

The following materials were used in the preparation of this case, in addition to observation and personal interviews.

The complete compendium of the Congress papers is published by World Wide Publications, 1313 Hennepin Avenue, Minneapolis, Minn. 55403, entitled *Let the Earth Hear His Voice,* edited by J. D. Douglas, copyright 1975 World Wide Publications.

Schaeffer, Francis A. *He Is There and He Is Not Silent.* Tyndale House Publishers, 1973.
Winter, Ralph, ed. *The Evangelical Response to Bangkok.* South Pasadena, Calif.: William Carey Library, 1973.

17

The World Council of Churches
Fifth Assembly (A.D. 1975)

Philip Potter climbed the plant-decked ramp to the Kenyatta Conference Center. Inside, native mahogany latticework enhanced the
decor, while on the floor of the center, men and women from over
one hundred nations were talking in small groups or sitting reading
through multitudinous papers. The dark-skinned West Indian General Secretary of the World Council of Churches slipped into his
chair, reflecting on the events of preceding days at this Fifth Assembly of the World Council and hoping that the few days remaining
would bring new movement toward the conciliar fellowship he so
desired, and toward the increased participatory commitment and
financial support the WCC so desperately needed from the churches.
Would the Section reports the delegates were now studying reaffirm
present policies and programs or demand new directions? Had the
troublesome relationship between evangelism and social action been
addressed with contemporary theological understanding and pragmatic insight? Had progress been made in dealing with the difficult
issues of contextualizing the Christian message and dialogue with
other religions? Had the Assembly adequately interpreted the conference theme, "Jesus Christ Frees and Unites"? Had the various
new and needy constituencies within the member churches and
represented by the advisers received appropriate hearing and response? Was significant progress being made toward Christian unity
at the deepest levels of shared worship and sacrament? What role
could he, as General Secretary, play in the days and months ahead?

This case study was prepared by Professor Jack Rogers of Fuller Theological Seminary
and students under his supervision: Roberta Hestenes, Kirk Kestler, Jim Reeve, Nate
Showalter, Bucky Sydnor, and Jean Wilson. It is intended as a basis for class discussion
rather than to illustrate either effective or ineffective handling of a situation.

The Composition and Context of the Assembly

Colorful native dress was mingled with Western business attire in the flower- and fountain-filled plaza of the sprawling Kenyatta Conference Center when the Fifth Assembly of the World Council of Churches met in Nairobi, Kenya, November 23 to December 13, 1975. Over two thousand persons gathered at this convocation of Protestant and Orthodox leaders representing more than 500 million Christians on six continents. Seven hundred and forty-seven of them were official delegates—80 percent at their first Assembly and 40 percent laity. The 75 delegates under age thirty and the more than 150 women gave these groups their most significant Assembly representation to date. In addition there were some 120 advisers, including 10 Roman Catholic and 10 Evangelical representatives, numerous official observers, a 250-member WCC staff, and a large press corps.

They had assembled to explore the theme "Jesus Christ Frees and Unites." The Swahili translation of "Freedom" and "Unity"—*Uhuru* and *Harambee*—had also been the rallying cry of Kenyan nationalists in their struggle against British dominance, thus underscoring one of the many concerns before the Assembly—the struggle for liberation and justice. There were also the issues of racism, women's rights, ecology, finances, hunger, and missions. Further, the Council's founding father, W. A. Visser 't Hooft, said: "If the meeting does not produce a new sense of purpose and dynamism, the Council will be in trouble. It is time the churches stop looking at the Council as a sort of fringe phenomenon."

The declining importance of the WCC to its member churches was reflected in the financial woes of the world organization. Meanwhile, the Council itself had been criticized for its "selective indignation" in heavily attacking the United States while ignoring human rights violations elsewhere. The presence of the Russian Orthodox in the Council (since 1961) was felt to have aggravated this lack of "even-handedness."

On another front, some evangelically oriented churchmen were deeply disturbed by the overwhelming commitment of WCC staff and resources to social action and alleged nonmissionary activities. In contrast, some Africans were demanding a temporary "moratorium" on foreign mission activity. Meanwhile, still other delegates were concerned with defining the meaning and purpose of dialogue with other faiths.

The Assembly had a full agenda as the delegates and other participants poured into the Kenyatta Center on that Sunday evening in November.

The Road to Nairobi

The contemporary ecumenical movement began with the World Missionary Movement of the last century, which climaxed in the World Missionary Conference held in Edinburgh in 1910. This interdenominational meeting of missionary society representatives became a major stimulus of ecumenical activity, culminating in the First Assembly of the World Council of Churches convening in 1948 in Amsterdam.

Another significant organization to come out of the Edinburgh meeting was the International Missionary Council in 1921, which then merged with the WCC in 1961 to become the WCC's Commission on World Mission and Evangelization (CWME). Its purpose was "to further the proclamation to the whole world of the Gospel of Jesus Christ to the end that all men may believe in Him and be saved."

By the time of the Fourth Assembly of the World Council of Churches at Uppsala in 1968, the shape of world events was producing significant response in the Council and its activities. The Vietnam war, the youth rebellion, emerging nations, and racial strife all had their effect. Feelings of anti-Americanism permeated the Assembly, whose overall emphasis focused on humanization and development in the social and economic spheres.

The CWME scheduled its 1973 world meeting in Bangkok to discuss "Salvation Today." Those hoping for a more traditionally oriented evangelistic thrust were grievously disappointed, for salvation was defined primarily in "this-worldly," socioeconomic terms. Many participants were disturbed by what they felt to be an almost manipulative control of the conference by WCC's Geneva office. Others, though, were glad to see this large Christian body firmly committed at last to meeting the needs of their fellow human beings in the name of Christ.

Meanwhile, another body of Christians was at work. In the summer of 1974, four thousand Evangelicals from around the world met at Lausanne for an International Congress on World Evangelization. This body issued the Lausanne Covenant, which declared:

Evangelism itself is the proclamation of the historical, biblical Christ as Savior and Lord, with a view to persuading people to come to him personally and be reconciled to God.

The Congress carefully distinguished between evangelism and social action, salvation and political liberation, but nevertheless affirmed social action as a Christian duty and a necessary expression of obedience to Christ. Many Lausanne participants, as leaders in member churches of the WCC, were hopeful that Lausanne would have a positive effect on the upcoming Nairobi Assembly.

The year 1974 also brought evangelistic emphasis at the Roman Catholic Synod of Bishops in Rome, as they explored "Evangelization in the Modern World." A similar emphasis was present at the Orthodox Consultation on "Confessing Christ Today" in Bucharest.

As Nairobi drew near, the more than 271 WCC member churches selected their delegates. The 121-member Central Committee, commissions, and work groups responsible for the continuing work and activities of the Council devoted time to preparation for the Assembly.

The General Secretary, Philip Potter, experienced a heightened sense of anticipation as the delegates assembled in Nairobi to begin their work.

M. M. Thomas, Moderator of the Central Committee

The first major address to the Assembly was given by Madathilparampil M. Thomas, moderator of the Central Committee.

A leader in the Mar Toma Church of India, a church that traced its heritage proudly back to Thomas the Apostle, M. M. Thomas had served as Moderator since Uppsala. His appointment had been noted as a sign of the growing shift within the World Council away from European dominance. Thomas was strongly committed to the growing "worldly" focus of the WCC, taking very seriously the view that "the Church and the world exist for each other in the gospel." During his years with the WCC many observers had noted that of the traditional WCC concerns—mission, unity, and service—the latter had become increasingly prominent with a growing emphasis on the needs of the Third World. The definition of the task of "unity" had expanded to include the needs, not just of a divided church, but increasingly of a divided humanity.

As Thomas rose to speak, he knew well the disparity between the WCC's broader understandings of the church's mission and the concern of some to narrow and limit the arena of WCC involvement. As he gave the Moderator's report to the Assembly, he attempted to present a theological understanding of the past actions and present challenges facing the Assembly.

With Roman Catholic observers looking on, Thomas spoke of his great regret that the Roman Catholic Church was not officially a part of the WCC. A second regret was the inability of WCC members to enjoy together eucharistic fellowship where all could join in the common cup and bread of Jesus Christ.

Thomas moved beyond these future agenda items, however, to address what he saw as the central concern of the present Assembly —how the contemporary ecumenical movement was to relate to the unity, evangelistic mission, and justice programs of the church.

Thomas sketched for the delegates his view that the contemporary realities of the secular world—rapid social change, diverse cultures, different religions and conflicting ideologies, the world of poverty and the awakening poor, the world of national and racial revolts and of movements for social liberation—called for new understandings and responses on the part of the church to help mankind find "the unity that it is seeking in so many ways."

In this light, Thomas traced what he saw as a radical change in the concept and form of world evangelism. He declared himself especially impressed with a new consensus understanding of evangelism. He spoke of the new "theological convergence" arising from Bangkok, Lausanne, Rome, and Bucharest. He quoted from key documents to demonstrate that all ecumenically concerned churches and groups recognize the positive relation between evangelism and Christian social responsibility. Within this common understanding, he sought to define the target of the gospel as not simply the individual person needing redemption.

> People are not isolated individuals; they are social beings, inextricably related to the structures of nature, history and cosmos through which they express the creativity of their freedom as well as the sin of self-love and self-righteousness. Persons, society and cosmos interpenetrate one another in the unity of human existence. Therefore if salvation from sin through divine forgiveness is to be truly and fully personal, it must express itself in the renewal of these relationships and structures. Such renewal is not merely a consequence but an essential element of the conversion of whole human beings.

Thomas turned next to touch an even more difficult question facing the WCC—dialogue with those outside the Christian faith. What was the point of dialogue—understanding or conversion? Are all persons ultimately saved? Is God at work equally in all religions? How is the church to relate to other faiths? Bangkok had refused to limit the saving presence of God to the church. While acknowledging that Christians enter the dialogue with other religions from the starting point of the centrality of the crucified and risen Jesus Christ, yet Christians are to be "keenly open to discover what He [God] is doing among people of other faiths." Thomas called for the Assembly to move beyond the Bangkok position to discover a genuine theology of dialogue, making a greater effort to "discern how Christ is at work in other faiths." Affirming that "Christ holds all things together now (Col. 1:17)," he called for a "Christ-centered syncretism."

> Acknowledging the common humanity given in Christ, can we not work with men of all religions for a secular human culture and community, and even for a secular humanism, open to insights from all religions and ideologies evaluated in the light of and informed by the true manhood of Jesus Christ?

As Thomas concluded, Potter wondered, Would Thomas' definition of evangelism and dialogue be the central notes or would more restrictive definitions impact the Assembly? Only the coming days would tell.

Robert McAfee Brown's Keynote Address

Tuesday afternoon, November 25, Californian Robert McAfee Brown rose to deliver the keynote address of the Assembly, "Who Is This Jesus Who Frees and Unites?" As a committed Christian, he had long been both a civil rights and political activist while a professor at Stanford University. Brown had wrestled seriously with the appropriateness of his own role as a white, American, middle-class male standing before a worldwide community of Christians. Many of those Christians, he felt, had suffered as a result of U.S. actions in the world. A narrowly parochial definition of Jesus Christ would simply not be adequate to the historical moment. So, as he presented his talk, he sought to challenge and stretch various of the limiting categories often used in talking of Jesus Christ. To those who defined Christ as social liberator, he spoke of Christ the personal redeemer; to those who would narrowly limit Christ to personal Savior, he spoke of Christ as the suffering servant who is present in the struggle for social justice and freedom. Then he moved to the thesis of his speech.

> Among the many claims made about Jesus Christ, on which shall we focus our attention? Our Assembly theme gives us some direction. . . . Nairobi describes Jesus as the one who Frees and Unites—Jesus the Liberator, Jesus the Unifier. As I shall suggest later, I believe that we cannot truly put those claims together unless we insert between them a claim that Jesus is also the Divider. As Jesus *liberates* us, we are required to face the poten-

tial *divisions* that liberation brings, so that we can move toward a truer *unity* than would otherwise be possible.

As a liberator, Jesus "frees us from . . . false securities," "for the possibility of seeing the world through eyes other than our own," and "for struggle with and on behalf of those others, who are the poor and dispossessed." But he also divides: those who are committed to him from those who are not; those who see him as a personal savior from those who see him as a political savior; those who will be liberated by him from their oppressors.

Finally, however, he is the Unifier. Jesus did not come "that all may be divided." He came "that all may be one."

The great surprise came when Brown spoke of confession and repentance, identifying himself as part of a group that needed to confess and repent. To mark the seriousness of his own belief that even language can be oppressive, he delivered the last part of his address in Spanish, embodying in practice his desire to work for a new unity in the Christian community, a unity to be found through confession and forgiveness.

> Mutual confession and forgiveness will be important ways in which we respond to Jesus the Unifier. For out of common *repentance* can come the beginnings of a new common *obedience.*

Many listeners were surprised at the *mea culpa* of the renowned theologian. Others rejoiced that the traditional arrogance and imperialism of the Western churches was being broken by the power of the gospel of Jesus.

Report of the General Secretary, Philip Potter

Early on Wednesday, November 26, Dr. Philip Potter stood before the Assembly. The fifty-four-year-old Methodist West Indian was born in Haiti of a devout Protestant mother and a Roman Catholic father. Interested in the church's mission even as a boy, he went on to theological training in Jamaica and advanced work at London University.

As a student, Potter was impressed with Barth's neo-orthodoxy and took to heart Reinhold Niebuhr's maxim that the Christian should live life with the Bible in one hand and the newspaper in the other. Potter's college involvement in the Student Christian Movement eventually brought him to the first WCC Assembly in 1948. He was appointed to the Youth Department Committee and became its chairman in 1954. Six years later he became the British Methodist

Missionary Society's field secretary for Africa and West Indies. In 1967 he returned to the WCC to serve as CWME director and five years later became the Council's General Secretary.

In 1974, Potter, as administrative head of the World Council, had been invited to Rome to address the Synod of Bishops of the Roman Catholic Church on their theme "Evangelization in the Modern World." He had seen his task as strengthening the links between the Council and the Vatican. He had attempted not only to point out their common call in regard to evangelism but also to point the way toward greater renewal and unity between these two great Christian bodies.

Now at Nairobi, a different task faced him, and the way would not be smooth. His own General Secretary's report would be followed that morning by a grim financial report. Potter felt that he must address not only this issue but also some of the other criticisms the WCC had received in the last years. He desired to demonstrate the legitimacy of the many worthwhile programs and causes the Council had supported in the name of Christ. He was also concerned for a new sense of belonging, community, and mutual obligation among member churches.

In his report Potter shared some of his reflections on the nature and task of the World Council and some of the challenges presented to the WCC by the events of the world.

> If we no longer say, as confidently as some years ago, that the world provides the agenda for the Church, we can at least assert that it is in discerning what God has been doing in his world that we have been given our marching orders to do what we have done.

He therefore attempted to trace some of the significant trends which had recently influenced both the content and style of the World Council's work.

The most striking trend, he noted, was that all major issues—social, economic, environmental, racial, sexist, or political—have become global and interrelated. The most serious threat, perhaps, was the widening gap between the rich and the poor. This gap was the direct effect of the prevailing world economic order, based on survival of the fittest and manipulated by the powerful. Such problems must be understood and tackled globally. He urged the Assembly to realize the "urgent need for mobilizing world Christian forces to meet them. That is precisely what the World Council of Churches has tried to do in the last seven years." Potter thus openly faced the criticism these efforts had elicited:

Many have questioned this preoccupation as diverting the WCC and the ecumenical movement away from its proper task of working for church unity and a true confession of faith in Christ. But when we speak of conflicts with nations, threats to human survival, racism, and violations of human rights, we are not talking about abstractions. We are addressing ourselves to human beings who create and operate them. The focus is on the human race itself—men and women, singly and corporately. We are talking about human sin in all its protean forms. And that is what our biblical faith is about.

In response to another criticism Potter answered those who call for "evenhandedness" in the Council's denunciation of those nations which violate human rights. He charged them with having ideological motivations that "mask a longing to escape the particular challenges" facing the churches.

Shifting to the constitutional matters which would occupy the Assembly, the General Secretary focused on his own questions about the Council's purposes and future. The Assembly would have to decide whether the proposed statement of purpose adequately expressed the requirements of both the WCC and the member churches.

Looking toward the future with these proposed goals in mind, Potter then delineated some of the consequences for the ecumenical movement. First, he was deeply concerned at the gap between the Council and the churches. Every Assembly, he said, had repeatedly emphasized that the credibility of the movement depended on active engagement of every church and congregation. The time had come to stop talking and to work out ways of "partnership in obedience." Secondly, the present financial resources were inadequate to meet the varied needs and present demands. Priorities must be worked out from both a global and a particular perspective. Thirdly, the interrelatedness of functions and purposes of the WCC and the churches ought to mean an interrelatedness of financial resources. He warned, "We are facing the possibility of becoming a fellowship of penury," but saw this as a challenge to reconsider priorities and pool resources. Then the program and budget of the WCC would be the concern of every church and vice versa.

This Assembly will have failed in its purpose if we do not advance to a new covenant relationship between the member churches at all levels of their life and the World Council at all levels of its activities.

Bishop Arias: "That the World May Believe"

On Thursday afternoon, November 27, the attention of the entire Assembly was focused on the subject of evangelism. For this fifth plenary session, Mortimer Arias had been chosen as speaker. Nearly two years before the Nairobi Assembly, Arias had been elected to a second four-year term as Bishop of the Evangelical Methodist Church in Bolivia.

During his first term as bishop, Arias had reported a doubling of Methodist membership in this Bolivian denomination. Uruguayan by birth, he had since become a naturalized Bolivian citizen, and had served as a pastor for thirty years before assuming responsibility as bishop in Bolivia's small Evangelical Methodist Church, still an "associate member" of the World Council. The fifty-two-year-old South American had distinguished himself internationally for his interest in evangelism, and for his leadership in a strategy of mission that combined social action with the more traditional concepts of evangelism.

Taking his text from John's Gospel (John 17:21), Bishop Arias entitled his speech, "That the World May Believe." He reminded the Assembly that its ecumenical endeavor had been born in a missionary movement, and declared that evangelization would be the "test" of the Fifth Assembly, "called together to make the most daring missionary and evangelistic affirmation that can be made in the world today: 'Jesus Christ Frees and Unites.' "

Going on to chide the Council for falling short of its evangelistic calling, for not always remaining true to what Potter had identified in Rome as "the test of [the World Council's] ecumenical vocation," Arias nevertheless boldly acclaimed "the missionary and evangelistic potential of all that the WCC has been doing through us and in our name." He identified as "mission" a wide variety of social programs sponsored by the ecumenical council, and listed them specifically as "an integral part of true evangelism in the world today."

The next paragraph of the bishop's speech presented a sharp shift of focus, surprising both to conservative listeners and to social activists:

> [At times] we have allowed ourselves to be impelled by an activism that owed more to fashionable slogans than to adequate biblical and theological reflection. And above all we must admit with shame that evangelism has been the Cinderella of the WCC, at least to judge by the extent to which it appears in its structure, where it figures by nothing more than one office with a single occupant, in a sub-structure which is itself merely part

of a unit, and with no more than a monthly letter by which to communicate with the churches of the whole world.

Bishop Arias then went on to give a five-pronged strategy for the next five years of World Council activity. One of those points was "to make more visible and functional the influence of mission and evangelism within the movement as a whole." As the core of his proposed strategy, the Methodist bishop outlined what he called a "holistic or integral approach" to evangelism. Quoting from a Bangkok document, Arias defined this approach as one in which "social justice, personal salvation, cultural affirmation, church growth, are all seen as integral parts of God's saving acts."

"Evangelism must also be contextual," insisted Arias in the second major section of his address. Both the method and the message in evangelism must be relevant to the culture of the receptor. This point Arias illustrated by citing the experience of his church in Bolivia, in a scheme of evangelism which attempted to incorporate this concern for contextuality, as well as the holistic or integral approach.

Arias next spoke of the cost in commitment of evangelizing the "2.7 billion who do not know Christ." He also spoke of the need for renewal, but cautioned that "renewal does not come *before* mission but *in* mission. It will not come through study and reflection alone, but through practical action which includes reflection in action and prayer. We must not give in to the temptation to perfectionism; we must take risks, we must commit ourselves to the gospel."

Finally Arias addressed the tension between *local* evangelism, growing out of the community and being communicated person to person, and a *universal* demand "that the world may believe." The Bolivian bishop then reminded the delegates that while the gospel is intended for the whole world, it is also clear that "God has his time which is not our time." He exhorted his audience:

> We must not fall into either guilty resignation or frantic activism. We must know how to pray and hope in God, and act according to the strength and wisdom he gives us. . . . Many of us today hear the heartrending cry of those whose human rights are violated. Is it not a basic right of every human being to know God's purpose for his life which was revealed in Jesus Christ?

Stott's Response

Three Assembly participants had been asked to respond to Bishop Arias' address. The last of the respondents was John Stott, one of the officially invited "Evangelical observers" at Nairobi, and moderator of the Lausanne Assembly of the previous year. When the other two respondents had finished, the time allotted for the plenary session was more than exhausted. The delegates were tired, but the moderator allowed the tall Anglican rector his scheduled ten minutes.

Stott was precise and to the point. He welcomed Arias' remarks, but doubted that they were representative of the World Council's position on evangelism. "It seems to many of us that evangelism has now become largely eclipsed," said Stott with reference to the ecumenical council, "by the quest for social and political liberation."

In his carefully measured diction, Stott listed five concerns necessary to the World Council's recovery of a proper involvement in evangelism: (1) A recognition of the lostness of man, (2) confidence in the gospel of God, (3) conviction about the uniqueness of Jesus Christ, (4) a sense of urgency about evangelism, and (5) a personal experience of Jesus Christ. Then, in an addition to his prepared text, Stott gave an appeal as his final word to the Assembly:

We are all aware of the wide gap of confidence and credibility that exists today between many ecumenical leaders and Evangelicals—if you like, between Geneva and Lausanne. What can be done about this gap? Ecumenical leaders genuinely question whether Evangelicals have a heartfelt commitment for social action. We Evangelicals say we have. But, I personally recognize that we've got to supply more evidence than we have.

On the other hand, Evangelicals genuinely question whether the World Council of Churches has any longer a heartfelt commitment to worldwide evangelization. They say they have, but I beg this Assembly to supply more evidence that this is so.

The genteel English bachelor sat down to a thunderous applause. The Assembly seemed to be rendering a kind of emotional verdict to Stott's critique and call for commitment, and that in spite of the lateness and fatigue of the hour.

Political Tensions

Throughout the Assembly critical questions were discussed and debated. At times affairs took on a political cast. Jamaica's Prime Minister Michael Manley delivered a scathing denunciation of capitalism which brought strong reaction from many Americans. Some were particularly concerned at the effect on raising support for the WCC, since three fourths of its finances came (about equally) from "capitalist" West Germany and the United States.

An unexpected development came during discussion of the recent Helsinki Agreement (a U.S.-U.S.S.R. concord on control of Eastern Europe and guarantee of human rights). A Swiss move from the floor specifically to censure the U.S.S.R. for human rights violations caught Moderator Thomas off guard; the unprecedented censure was swiftly passed by the delegates. Alarmed at potential Soviet reaction as well as possible reprisals against the Orthodox churchmen, an American delegate made a parliamentary objection. Thomas hastily called for a tea break, during which furious caucusing resulted in a delay and a compromise measure. Many felt that this move threatened WCC integrity, since the West could be criticized with impunity but not the Soviets. Others, however, felt that the delicate position of the Russian churchmen called for sensitivity. World Council officials breathed a sigh of relief at the outcome, in spite of severe criticism of the parliamentary maneuvering.

A Third World emphasis at the Assembly was prominent, as expected, but did not become the explosive issue anticipated. Some felt Brown's keynote address, with its "confession" of Western "sins," had a defusing effect. Others noted with approval the number of Third World plenary speakers and the time devoted to the subjects of oppression and liberation. Liberian Anglican Canon Burgess Carr called for a "moratorium" on Western mission funds and personnel in Africa, in order that a truly African theology might be developed. However, the Africans were far from united on the issue, since many churches felt deeply dependent on outside support.

Work-Study Groups:
Section 1, "Confessing Christ Today"

In addition to the plenary addresses and business meetings, significant time was devoted to the six Assembly Sections, which covered such topics as confessing Christ, unity, community, and structures of injustice. To the amazement of the planners, over half the delegates chose Section 1, "Confessing Christ Today." Only three hundred could be accommodated. Each of the Section's five work-study groups met frequently for study and discussion; a theological adviser was appointed for each group to draft their subsection report reflecting the group discussion and consensus. Participants who had been at Bangkok appreciated the methodological shift. This time no prewritten draft held the delegates to a "Geneva agenda," and the report could be genuinely reflective of the participants. In fact, when prominent German theologian Jürgen Moltmann proceeded to draft his "own" report in disregard of his group's discussion and consensus, he was criticized and asked to rework the draft. Representing a cross section of Christian thought, the Section advisers also included William Lazareth, American Lutheran theologian; Robert Moss, United Church of Christ; Albert van den Heuvel, Dutch Reformed; Tom Stransky, Paulist priest; Mortimer Arias, the Bolivian Methodist bishop; and David Hubbard, president of Fuller Theological Seminary. The preliminary drafts, worked over by the groups, were twice submitted to the Assembly for discussion and amendment, then in the last week a final version was to be submitted for adoption.

The report of Section 1 contained many varied affirmations, confessions, and challenges, as well as twenty-one "recommendations to the churches" for evangelism, renewal, and service. The Section basically affirmed the distinction made previously at Lausanne between salvation and service, while maintaining the necessity of both.

> Through the power of the cross, Christ promises God's righteousness and commands human justice.... Christians are therefore called to engage in both evangelism and social action. We are commissioned to proclaim the gospel of Christ to the end of the earth. Simultaneously, we are commanded to struggle to realize God's will for peace, justice, and freedom throughout society.

Liberation from sin and evil should be limited neither to the political and social dimensions nor to the private and eternal dimensions. "We regret all divisions in thinking and practice between the personal and the corporate dimensions." Although involvement in struggles for justice and freedom liberates confession from "mere verbalism," still "one must name the Name"; "without clear confession of Christ our discipleship will not be recognized."

Section 1 also sought to deal with the cultural issue. Confessing Christ should be done as specifically as possible with regard to cultural setting, for Christ meets us in our own cultural contexts. "We have found this confession of Christ . . . not only a mutually inspiring exchange, but also a mutually corrective one" with a potential for transforming cultures and individuals. Many structures of society—economic, racial, sexist, and institutional—obscure the image of Christ, particularly Christ the Unifier, yet Christ "is not alien to any culture." The church must be aware of its own oppressive structures, as well as those it opposes in society.

> The report expressed its concept of dialogue: While we cannot agree on whether or how Christ is present in other religions, we do believe that God has not left himself without witness in any

generation or any society. . . . While we oppose any form of syncretism, we affirm the necessity for dialogue with men and women of other faiths and ideologies as a means of mutual understanding and practical cooperation.

Dealing with the essential corporate dimension of Christian confession—"being converted to Christ necessarily includes membership in the confessing body of Christ," the report focused on unity in eucharistic fellowship. "This communion of the spirit finds its primary aim and ultimate purpose in the eucharistic celebration and the glorification of the Triune God." Worship, especially the eucharist, is seen as the means through which Christian communities open themselves to God and his creation, thus breaking down divisions. "It is our lasting shame and pain that we have not overcome our divisions at the Lord's table."

The Section 1 participants also boldly affirmed the call to proclaim the whole gospel. The task of evangelization had been entrusted to the whole church, not just a gifted few. Obedience to God and solidarity with the human family demand that God's love be proclaimed and demonstrated to the whole world. Since world evangelization begins at the congregational level, it implies for the churches a need for "repentance, renewal, and commitment to visible unity." Nor should the church hesitate in confessing its faith to others because of

misunderstanding our belief in the uniqueness and finality of Jesus Christ as "arrogant doctrinal superiority," and not understanding it as humble and obedient stewardship.

Section 1 ended its report with a challenge. No longer must the churches hesitate. Even though theological and methodological problems remain, a sense of the urgency of evangelism must be recovered:

We need to recover the sense of urgency. Questions about theological definitions there may be. Problems of precise implementation will arise. But neither theoretical nor practical differences must be allowed to dampen the fires of evangelism.

Reflection

In some ways it had been a difficult Assembly for General Secretary Potter. Some participants had described him as brusque and irritable during the Assembly, but he carried a heavy burden. As parliamentarian at several sessions, he had found the floor fights painful and divisive. In response to continued British criticism of the Council's controversial antiracism program, Potter had charged on Friday night's BBC broadcast that the British had "established a racist system wherever they have gone" in the world. He was glad that the Council's program for combating racism had remained intact in spite of the current economic crunch.

In front of him lay a sheaf of papers—the final drafts of the various section reports. Soon they would go to the floor for final approval. The reports were in keeping with his own call for participation, yet he wondered: Would they reaffirm present WCC policies and programs or would they call for dramatically new directions? How would the Assembly respond to the popularity of the Section 1 theme "Confessing Christ Today"? Had the troublesome relationship between evangelism and social action been addressed with theological understanding and pragmatic insight? Would the report of Section 1 provide an adequate basis on which to deal with the difficult issue of adapting the Christian message to a plurality of cultural contexts? Could dialogue with other religions go ahead? And in what form?

Potter mused on the Assembly theme, "Jesus Christ Frees and Unites." Would the election of two women among the six Presidents of the Council and more women, youth, and representatives of developing nations to the Central Committee be perceived as a significant response to their needs? Would the constituencies which Roman Catholic and Evangelical advisers represented be drawn to closer fellowship with the WCC? Would WCC member churches be encouraged toward the increased participation and financial support which the world organization so desperately needed? And, at a deeper level, when would Christians be fully united in eucharistic fellowship in the bread and cup of Jesus Christ? What role could he, as General Secretary, play in the days and months until the next Assembly seven years hence? All these thoughts churned in Philip Potter's mind as he waited for the meeting to begin.

BIBLIOGRAPHY

Resources principally used in preparing this case included mimeographed copies of addresses distributed to the World Council of Churches Fifth Assembly participants, newspaper and magazine reports, and interviews of persons present at the Assembly.